CW00434466

Raghava R. Menon studied music in the g
Pandit V.A. Kashalkar, one of the oldest
Digambar Palusker. For many years he w........ .. . .iations
executive. Subsequently he was associated with the University of the
State of New York. He has also been a visiting professor at several
European universities. Mr Menon has written and published several
book-reviews, short stories and articles on music in several newspapers
and magazines in India and abroad including the *Australian Journal
of Politics and History* and the *Saturday Review*. He has also published
several books on music including *Discovering Indian Music, A Journey
into Raga* (which has been translated into German, French and Rus-
sian), a biography of K.L. Saigal named *The Pilgrim of the Swara* and
is presently a music critic for Indian music in the *Times of India* and
for Western music in the *Hindustan Times*.

Raghava R. Menon

The Penguin Dictionary
of
Indian Classical Music

PENGUIN BOOKS

PENGUIN BOOKS
Published by the Penguin Group
Penguin Books India Pvt. Ltd, 11 Community Centre, Panchsheel Park, New
Delhi 110 017, India
Penguin Group (USA) Inc., 375 Hudson Street, New York, New York 10014,
USA
Penguin Group (Canada), 90 Eglinton Avenue East, Suite 700, Toronto,
Ontario, M4P 2Y3, Canada (a division of Pearson Penguin Canada Inc.)
Penguin Books Ltd, 80 Strand, London WC2R 0RL, England
Penguin Ireland, 25 St Stephen's Green, Dublin 2, Ireland (a division of Penguin
Books Ltd)
Penguin Group (Australia), 250 Camberwell Road, Camberwell, Victoria
3124, Australia (a division of Pearson Australia Group Pty Ltd)
Penguin Group (NZ), 67 Apollo Drive, Rosedale, North Shore 0632, New
Zealand (a division of Pearson New Zealand Ltd)
Penguin Group (South Africa) (Pty) Ltd, 24 Sturdee Avenue, Rosebank,
Johannesburg 2196, South Africa

Penguin Books Ltd, Registered Offices: 80 Strand, London WC2R 0RL,
England

First published by Penguin Books India 1995

Copyright © Raghava R. Menon 1995

All rights reserved

10 9 8 7 6

Typeset in *New Century Schoolbook* by Digital Technologies and Printing
Solution, New Delhi
Printed at Anvi Composers, New Delhi

To
Rukmini
for her steadfastness

Acknowledgements

I would like to gratefully acknowledge the help of the Sangeet Natak Academy and the Madras Music Academy for various kinds of assistance given to me in compiling this dictionary. Many discussions with the late Ustad Zahiruddin Dagar, Pandit Mallikarjun Mansur, Umayalapuram Shivaraman, invaluable references from the works of B. Subba Rao and Dr V. Raghavan and the works of Bhathkande and Pandit Ratanjanker, the main publications of the journal of the Indian Musicological Society, Baroda, the journal of the National Centre for the Performing Arts, Professor Sambamurty's invaluable *Encyclopaedia of South Indian Music and Musicians* and the articles of S. Bandopadhyaya have all contributed to the making of this volume. Most of all I would like to express my gratitude to Ms Animol Varghese for typing the manuscript.

Introduction

In the Indian musical tradition, it is not easy to conceive of a dictionary of music. Whatever can be said about Indian classical music, or put together as a compendium of meanings, would have little true value. Musicians are quick to challenge those who theorize about music, asking them to sing and demonstrate their knowledge of the art instead. This was cruelly brought to my attention in a meeting in which the late Ustad Nazir Zahiruddin Dagar was present. There was an M.Phil student of music, sitting before us, failing miserably in his efforts to tune his tanpura. The Ustad turned to me and said: 'Who is this mahapurush who has an M.Phil in music but is not able to distinguish the strings of his tanpura from the pegs?'

This is the predicament that textbook knowledge and information about music produces. A lifetime offers precious little time for the pursuit of art. Of that, the hours spent on seeking information and bookish knowledge of music takes away from the student of music the time he could have spent on training to be a musician. The late B.C. Deva once asked the maestro of the Patiala gharana, the great Bade Gulam Ali Khan, why Hindustani music cannot be standardized and made scientific. The Khan Saheb replied, 'It is scientific enough as its living greatness proves in each generation; for the rest, any knowledge about music is like knowledge about God, and my knowledge is as good as yours.'

Such an approach to life is not altogether an oriental aberration. There is a thought-provoking little incident which Christopher Isherwood relates in his Berlin stories.

He recalls the time when, while still a child, he used to marvel at the transformation in the colours of the woods when seen through the stained glass windows of a church in his neighbourhood. The grim German landscape glowed through the glass of the Virgin's garments in preternatural gamboges and burnt siennas, aquamarines and salmons. Later, after the war and after a college education, he returned to the same church still miraculously undamaged in spite of repeated Allied bombings, and peeped through the same stained glass of the windows. But instead of the colours of an Eden before the Fall, he now beheld only a mass of his own favourite adjectives. So it is with Indian music too. In learning the art of Indian classical music, words can become an impediment to the kind of transformations that are involved in mastering it. Its principal artistes always resist the attempt to obtain a too facile understanding of the art.

Then there is the problem of history—Indians are generally accused of not having enough of a historical sense. In music, more than in any other art, there is only the present. The leading edge of the art lies in its living exemplars. Its history is not a history of dates. It lies in an inspiration that transcends description except as felt experience. Such history as there is, is oral history, reborn each time it is related. This means that any kind of acceptable history would consist only of the actual experience of a period of time rarely more than three generations old. It is for this reason that as the decades pass, and the memory of a singer begins to diminish, there is an effort to resuscitate it. And so a great musician's memory is mythified and exalted to the level of magic and miracle. This is achieved by making a legend of the man. The great Mian Tansen is a case in point—a musician who, history would have us believe, could light lamps, cure sickness and stop marauding elephants in their tracks with the power of music. But while in most other cultures the desire to make a science of music was so great that tuning forks and the tempered scale were used to effect this, the Indian tradition has always resisted the impulse to make a logocentric art of music when it began as a phonocentric one.

The principal reason for this 'unscientific', sympathetic treatment of music is that the basic note in Indian music cannot be understood merely in terms of the pitch produced by a tuning fork. As a consequence, it has no tempered scale. The building brick of the Indian raga is the swara which is not a note but a human utterance. The effort, even when playing an instrument in the Indian classical tradition, is to approximate the human voice. It is as a voice that Indian music is heard and not as a sound. The note 'C' as a swara is not exactly the same as the note itself when rendered in the Indian classical style, its identical frequency notwithstanding. This difference is so essential in the experience of Indian music that no definition, however carefully constructed, can offer a true understanding of the nature of this principal ingredient of the art.

Though the Carnatic and the Hindustani are considered to be the two main traditions of Indian music, there is only one music in India—the music of the raga. The technique of making music through harmony and counterpoint and the assembling of many hundred instruments through vertical writing is what makes Western music Western, and it remains so whether the composer is German, Japanese or Papuan. Similarly, the music of the raga, whether Carnatic or Hindustani, is what makes Indian music Indian. All other differences are minor and localized when compared to the inspiration of the raga on which this music is based.

It is in the nature of the raga to make codifications and standardizations of the technical content of Indian music meaningless. For example, everyone knows that the raga lives and dies in the instant. Unlike a painting or a sculpture or any of the compositions of Western music which are all finished products, frozen in time, a raga does not exist until sung or played and only lives in the instant, dying as soon as it is born. This is one of the reasons why musicians resisted attempts to record the art when the recording industry was first established in the country. Once recorded, Indian musicians felt, music becomes a part of recollection and reminiscence. Indian classical music is a timeless art. It knows no age, it has no yesterdays or tomorrows, just as there are no old rivers, no old seas, nor an old wind.

The basic elements of music, such as the shruti, have no true existence outside the trained ear of the musician. When the great Bade Gulam Ali Khan sang the gandhara of Pilu or the gandhara of Darbari, it was his ear that indicated to him the feeling he wanted from his voice, and he had little concern with what they called that shruti, whether it had a name or none. He sang it to fulfil an inner obligation to the raga and gave it emotional colouring in order to give credibility to the words in which the raga was wrapped.

'The shruti,' according to Ustad Fariduddin Dagar, 'cannot exist on paper, however accurately calibrated, for its emotional content is beyond calculation, and without its emotional colouring it is only a note and not a swara. The swara exists in the ear of the musician as a feeling and not as a sound and it must match the word which gives it life in the bandish. So while it is true that someone invented the shruti veena and tuned each swara on it and all the twenty shrutis were incorporated, no one ever believed in it literally and no one would sing those shrutis without demeaning the raga and the bandish.'

This is where a one-to-one effort at providing meanings to words is so incomplete that the musical tradition has never attempted trying to put it all down. For example, take the word meend. This is one of the most communicative of the graces of Indian music. It could be defined as a portamento, that is a gliding movement from one note to another, without actually touching the notes in between. Obviously, for stringed instruments that are plucked, the meend is qualitatively different from the meend in a bowed instrument like the violin, the sarangi or the esraj. But these differences cannot be described on paper.

'But the meend,' Ustad Moinuddin Dagar once said, 'is actually an unconscious psychological act. For example, the pancham-rishabh meend in Raga Yeman, which is almost a cliche for the young student of music, is not just a passage on a scale, it is a reaching to the very end of life in the raga. Nothing kills the raga as applying rules of the book, and producing and reproducing the laws on which the raga is supposed to be based. The best thing is not to define it. Even a rudimentary musician would prefer to leave the rules undefined and rely on training his feelings about the raga and guide its laws towards incandescence.'

Then there is the tempi. The Western system puts metronome marks to indicate speed. In Indian classical music it is the language and structure of the bandish that determines the tempi. The vilambit and the madhya laya are dependent on the language and poetry of the bandish.

The problem in making a dictionary of Indian music is that no true musician will find much use for it. If he looks at it, it will be out of a curiosity to know how scholars will look above and below the truth in order to define its words and put down their meanings. As for colleges and schools where students have to appear for qualifying examinations, a volume in the style of a dictionary would be a handy alibi to possess. A dictionary makes it easy for these students of theory to forget that the words and the laws of music came long after the art had become part and parcel of life for centuries. The process of studying the grammar of music, categorizing concepts and defining them came much later. In fact, this process did not take place until the early years of this century, when the two doyens of the Hindustani music tradition, Pandit Vishnu Narayan Bhatkhande and Pandit Vishnu Digambar Palusker, attempted a systematic study of Hindustani music.

Indian classical music is solo whether Carnatic or Hindustani, in a sense in which Western classical music can never be. In Western music, an unaccompanied solo piano recital is not solo in the sense of Indian classical music. The pianist uses two hands and his two hands play like two separate musicians playing music together, the left hand playing notes that enrich and add a short vertical dimension to the melody played by the right hand. This technique of combining various notes which are in consonance and harmonically related to the main notes of melody is the basic ingredient of Western music and distinguishes it from the Indian classical system. On the other hand, in Indian classical music the instruments accompanying the performer, whether sarangi, violin, veena or any other, continues to keep the performance solo. For these accompaniments would always play on the same plane and in the same line as the main melody or raga.

Traditionally the absolute minimum supporting instruments required to make a Hindustani classical music concert possible are a tanpura and a tabla or pakhawaj. In a Carnatic music concert it would be a tanpura and a mridangam. Any further addition of sarangi or violin is mere prettification. For both the systems a tanpura provides the ground tonic note and the tabla or the mridangam provides the metric anchoring for the pace of the compositions and various intricate measures. The older schools of listeners, many of whom have transmitted this approach to several members of this generation, considered any instrument beyond the basic requirement mentioned earlier a needless distraction from the power and stoic austerity of the music. It can be likened to colouring a rock surface of a wall with emulsion paint. In more recent times the sarangi or harmonium has become a standard accompaniment to Hindustani classical music. In the Carnatic tradition the European violin is used as accompaniment. The Hindustani system rarely uses any other instrument apart from the tabla for its rhythmic needs. In the Carnatic tradition the ghatam, the kanjira and the morsing are common instruments of concert use.

The instruments of accompaniment in both systems of music have a descriptive but always derivative role, adding to the soloist's statements by actual extension or by innuendo. The accompaniment helps the soloist on, urging him to elaborate and expand further. This technique helps in layering and adding piquancy to meaning, thus enriching design. A concluding or an intermediate region of the concert is left open to the accompanists to show their skills within the larger context of the performance the soloist has established. While this practice has been standard for several decades in Carnatic music, the place of the tabla and sarangi or harmonium in Hindustani music has been, until very recent times, relatively minor.

The principal difference in the atmosphere of Carnatic and Hindustani music actually lies in the crucial differences between the two systems arising from the historical circumstances of their evolution. The Carnatic tradition is based on fully composed musical pieces called kritis which, like the sonata or the fugue, have certain well-established structures that fully elaborate the raga in all its emotional and textual ramifications. Thus the rendition of the kriti alone, as originally conceived by the composer, offers a complete picture of the raga, the rhythmic form of the kriti and the many mathematically related variations of the phrases of the lyric in play, in meditation and resolution.

A concert is fully expressed in a kriti in any raga. All the other inputs like alapana, neraval and swaraprastharas are rhythmic variations and play on scansion of the basic theme of the kritis which merely express several further aspects of tala, lyric and raga. The kritis of Carnatic music composed by the saint singers like Thyagaraja, Dikshitar, and Syama Shastri constitute familiar musical knowledge for the masses of South Indians even more than the Te Deum would be familiar to someone who lives in Salzberg. A Carnatic concert therefore offers a fully calibrated musical and emotional framework for concerts.

The Hindustani concert on the other hand is based more on the raga than on the original compositions. There is very little unanimity in the approach to traditional compositions, except in its fidelity to raga and to tala and certain qualities of gait and lyrical emphasis. The compositions which are called bandishes are actually little more than seeds from which a whole continent of ideas and musical theophanies has to be built, all of which lie in the mind and spirit of the performer and do not depend on the composer of the bandish. In many compositions even the name of the composer is not known—these are bandishes that have been handed down the ages as part of the oral tradition to which the music still belongs.

The kriti is a whole concert in the Carnatic context and if a performer does not want to add anything of his own mind to it, the concert would still be a memorable experience. It is like playing the polonaise in *A* on the piano, complete—no one is asking for anything more. In the Hindustani system the singing of the bandish is like showing you a bath tub full of water as a description of the Niagara. The Niagara must flow from the mind and spirit of the musician.

While there is a broad commonality in the nature of Indian classical music, there are other issues that make for diversity in the music traditions in India. For instance, Indian classical music is embodied in several Indian languages and dialects in word as well as spirit. Hindi, Bengali, Marathi, Tamil, Telugu, Sanskrit, Kannada, Brij, Bhojpuri, Malawi and Dingal, have all contributed to the art. And there are fundamental differences in the treatment of the music that grows out of the differences in these languages which reflect the differences in culture, history and regional traditions.

A dictionary of Indian music in English would have to find a median position, opting for the well-known and the more commonly used words and their meanings, and adopting a style of spelling that phonetically reproduces the sound of each word. The Sanskrit words are easy and even when a word is not in Sanskrit, most such words have a standard pronunciation based on the way they are written in the Devanagari script. Local differences abound and there are many variations of each term. It would be technically adequate each time to use any or all of these variants more or less at random so long as they sound the way they are heard or known.

In the case of ragas there are other problems. The ragas have to be selected keeping in mind of a personal predilection for a portable dictionary. What would be the criteria for selecting ragas? Handled more fully it would be less of a dictionary and more of an encyclopaedia. Consider the question of popularity. Popular where, would be an inevitable question. For example, the ragas Gaoti, Bhinna Shadja or even Kalavati—are these popular ragas? Yes, they are popular in some parts of the country. In Allahabad you would have less to do with Khambavati than in Bombay where it is fairly commonly sung. But if you have studied music or have been taught music, there are ragas you simply would have to learn for even the most elementary understanding of music. Musical training of say three years would involve learning a few of these most basic ragas. These have to be included in any volume that purports to be a dictionary of music. In any given slice of about twenty-five years of history, some ragas would be sung regularly and repeatedly. Each generation has its own ragas and those would then have to come into a listing of ragas, however superficial or casual their selection. At its very least, such a collection would go beyond a thousand ragas taking everything into account.

The gharanas would teach fewer ragas than the schools for they have to prove nothing except teach the ragas they believe they specialize in. The schools would teach more as far as numbers go. Schools would believe in substituting with quantity what you cannot provide in quality.

A thousand ragas including all the melakartas, the raginis and the thaats would be a hefty collection on its own and even then would not be complete as there are several styles of rendering these ragas. Several ragas are of recent origin, particularly in instrumental music, where new ragas come into being with greater frequency. These ragas have been largely omitted here as they are young and are yet to grow roots of their own, independent of their discoverer. Another dictionary some years later may have to cover these ragas. Among recent attempts the Pandit Amarnath volume of *Living Idioms* is a first rate book of reference dealing with the largely colloquial linguistic base of Hindustani music.

In any case, with each succeeding edition it would be necessary to incorporate the leading edge of the art as it travels, taking in its journey more and newer words and concepts in its passage through time.

Monsoons 1994   *Raghava R. Menon*
New Delhi

A

aa is the primary enunciation of a raga. It is also called the akar, the open-mouthed enunciation of *aa* as in bar. (See AKARASADHAKAM.)

Abali is a raga favoured by the Tallapakam musicians of the Carnatic school. The kriti *'payatandincheve'* in this raga is well known.

abhanga is a religiously inspired musical form and is commonly sung in Maharashtra. The three saints, Namadeva, Tukaram and Eknath were the original composers of the abhanga form. It shares certain characteristics with the KIRTANA of the Carnatic school. The Maharashtra rulers of Tanjore made abhangas popular in the south. There are sections in abhangas that correspond to the pallavi and charanam of a kriti and often these movements have identical musical notations.

abhava is produced when frequent repetitions of a phrase or a group of phrases destroys the appeal of the phrase or song and denatures its spirit.

Abheri is a janya raga derived from the melakarta Natabhairavi that corresponds to the Asavari thaat. This raga is similar in spirit to the Hindustani Raga Bhimpalasi. There is a raga called **Abhir** in the Hindustani tradition which is akin to Abheri in scale, but it is not often sung. The kriti that begins *'Nagumomu ganaleni'* of Thyagaraja is the only composition by the great saint in this raga. Syama Shastri's *'Ninu vina'* and Muthuswamy Dikshitar's *'Vinabheri'* are all beautiful compositions in this raga.

Abhinava Bharati is the famous commentary on Bharata's *Natya Shastra* written by Abhinava Gupta, a Kashmiri Brahmin, and one of Sanskrit literature's illustrious names.

abhog is the third movement of a composition in dhrupad or dhammar. It connotes one more line of lyric. (See DHATU.)

Abhogi is a janya raga of the twenty-second melakarta, Karaharapriya. Thyagaraja's 'Manasu nitapa sakti' and 'Nanu brova' and Gopalakrishna Bharati's 'Sabhaptikkuveru deivam' are beloved kritis in this raga. It is the equivalent of Abhogi Kanada in Hindustani music, which is a relatively new raga in the north. This belongs to the Kafi thaat. The bandish, 'Charana dhara aayee re' in Jhaptaal is widely sung.

abhyasa means repetition and practice in any raga so that its BAHUTWA swaras are practised to perfection.

abhyasa gana means music intended to exercise rather than produce feeling. The opposite of abhyasa gana is SABHA GANA which is a public performance. Thus abhyasa gana has all the principal elements of music—geeta, charana, swara prasthara —and is directed towards felicity with tala and swara. Concert training begins after this stage is over.

achala swara is the unmoving note. There are two such notes on the Indian scale. These are the SHAD JA, which is the tonic note, and its fifth, the PANCHAMA swara. They are the same as the *Do* and *So* of the solfege. These notes have no sharps or flats to them.

achyuta shadja is the tonic note or the shadja. This is differentiated from the chyuta shadja-nishada which is slightly lower in frequency when compared to the tonic shadja. If C is the frequency of an achyuta shadja, this frequency is reduced to 243/128 in the case of the chyuta shadja-nishada. The concept of shuddha shadja was introduced in Sarang Deva's time and was deemed to be the same as the achyuta shadja.

adambara is a drum used in war to help marching soldiers. It is used by drummers accompanying the army.

Adana is a very popular raga in Hindustani music. It belongs in the Asavari thaat. There is no raga by the same name in the south. The raga called Atthana bears certain similarities with the Hindustani Adana. It is a shadava-sampoorna raga.

Adarang is the *nom de plume* of Feroze Khan, a khayal composer and singer in the court of the last Mughal Badshah, Mohamed Shah 'Rangile' (1719–48) who was a great lover of music. Adarang and a contemporary and fellow court musician, SADARANG, composed several vilambit and dhrut khayals, many of which have become part of a very rich inheritence of the KHAYAL gayaki. The influence of Sufi mysticism is evident in his music. The name of Mohamed Shah, the patron of these two singers, is found in all the compositions in honour of their mentor.

adhama raga is a raga not suitable for musical compositions. Adhama means degraded, and therefore unsuitable for upliftment.

adhara shadja is the basic swara, the tonic, the fundamental note on which a raga is built. This is another term for the SHAD-JA.

Adi Panchama is a janya

raga derived from the raga Divyamani which is the forty-eighth melakarta.

adi raga is the first raga known to man. Shringara or love is believed to have inspired the first music, the first raga.

adi swara(s) are the first swaras among the most ancient in the Indian scale. These are known by the names udatta, anudatta and swarita of the Vedic hymns. Panini refers to these notes as adi swaras. They do not figure in contemporary music.

adi tala is the Chaturasra jati Triputa tala consisting of eight akshara kalas. (See TALA.)

aditya is a kind of flute in which the flute's blow holes and the first finger stop are separated by twelve angulas. An angula is about the distance that separates two fingers when stretched. It is found among tribal people whose flute is believed to be a direct descendant of the aditya.

aghati are cymbals used as percussion for dance and religious music referred to in the *Rig Veda*.

Agra gharana is one of the premier gharanas of Hindustani music. Its musicians are supposed to have descended from the line of Mian Tansen, down the line of his daughter, Saraswati. The Agra gharana's principal characteristic is the dhrupad-based alap. In the khayal of this gharana, the *nom tom* syllable helps distinguish the dhrupad style. The first movement of the khayal, the sthayi, is sung after the conclusion of the dhrupad-style alap. It has a fine chest register of voice production. The main singers of this gharana are Ustad Gulam Abbas Khan, Bhaskar Bua, Faiyaz Khan, Nathan Khan and Vilayat Hussein Khan.

Ahari is the other name of

the raga, **Ahiri,** mentioned in the venerable *Sangeeta Ratnakara.* It is a janya raga of the fourteenth melakarta, Vakulabharanam. This is a SANKIRNA raga.

ahat   (ahata) simply means audibility. It is the resistance of air in vibration that produces an audible sound. It belongs in the fundamental philosophic premise of the word NADA, where the audible part is called ahat and the inaudible, ANAHAT. Ahat music is classified under geeta, vadya and nritya.

Ahiri Todi is a janya raga of the eighth melakarta, Hanumatodi.

Ahobala is the author of the book, *Sangeeta Parijata,* written around the seventeenth century. He was the first known Indian musicologist who calibrated the value of swaras in terms of the lengths of stretched strings.

Ahori is a janya raga of the twentieth melakarta, Natabhairavi.

Airavati is a janya raga of the sixty-fourth melakarta, Subhapantuvarali.

akarasadhakam is a Sanskrit term and denotes the practice of music using the intonation, *aa.* This practice with the vocal chords up and down the scale gives roundness of tone, richness of timbre, transparency and strength to the voice. It is among the basic vocal exercises in Indian music. In Hindustani music the equivalent term is **akarasadhana**.

aksharakala is a unit of time in music. This is a relative, not an absolute measure. The vilambit laya (slow pace), the madhya laya (medium pace) and the dhruta laya (fast pace) are all subject to personal and subjective interpretation.

Alaiya Bilawal belongs to the Bilawal thaat and is

a morning raga. The Carnatic raga, **Bilahari**, bears a resemblance to Alaiya Bilawal of the Hindustani system.

alanghana is one of the two approaches which makes it possible to reveal the aspect of the raga known as BAHUTWA. Alanghana bahutwa indicates notes which are to be used with care in the elaboration of a raga.

alankar describes the decorative figures that adorn a raga. These are scale exercises that give a student a sense of the space and possibilities of a raga in terms of the figures it is capable of producing. Scarlatti's five finger exercises are a case in point. (See BRIHADDESI.)

alap is the opening out and spreading of the substance of a raga. It denotes the development of a raga through improvisation in such a way that the raga's form and spirit are revealed, while observing all the laws that govern the raga. When no words, syllables or mnemonics are used in alap, it is called anakshara alap. When a raga uses mnemonics to convey a verbal meaning, it is termed sakshara alap. A lot of the mnemonics used carry spiritual import, like *'Om Ananta Narayana'*. Alap is the richest area of music and is a sure index of a musician's musical, intellectual and spiritual capabilities. **Alapana** is the equivalent term in Carnatic music.

alapin is the fourth or the final shruti of the swara panchama in the twenty-two shruti theory of Bharata.

Alladiya Khan (1855-1946) was one of the greatest masters of the Jaipur-Atrauli gharana. Although a Muslim by birth, he wore the sacred thread of the Rajput Hindus. His prominent disciples were Munjhi Khan,

6

Burji Khan, Kesar Bai Kerkar, Bhaskar Bua Bhakle, Moghubai Kurdiker, the mother of Kishori Amonker, and Shanker Rao Sarnaik.

Allauddin Khan was among the most distinguished of musicians whose name is now identified with the Maihar gharana. He was one of the greatest sarod maestros. His guru was Rampur's Wazir Khan, a player of the been, identified with the Senia gharana. Later he settled down in Madhya Pradesh in the town of Maihar, which became synonymous with his name and the musical tradition he began. Through his shishya, Ravi Shankar, and son, Ali Akbar Khan, his name travelled all over the world. The Ustad came into prominence at the Lucknow Music Conference in 1924-25, where his sarod recitals made a prodigious impact, leaving listeners dumbfounded.

The Khan Saheb had a particular felicity with any instrument that he chose to play and formed the famous Maihar band, an ensemble of several instruments that played in unison. His daughter Annapurna Devi is one of the most distinguished surbahar players of our times and was at one time married to her father's shishya, Pandit Ravi Shankar. The Ustad was a remarkable example of intense sadhana in contemporary times. He died at the age of a hundred in 1972. Among his famous disciples were also Pannalal Ghosh, Nikhil Bannerjee and Timir Baran.

amad is the Urdu term for the skilfully calibrated entrance of the tabla into a tala cycle, meeting what is called the *sam*, which is the main forcefully accented beat of the tala cycle. The term also denotes the auspicious beginning of a performance. Traditionally this is done by invoking the blessings of Lord Ganesha. The amad is also called the SALAMI.

Aman Ali Khan was the originator of the Bhendi Bazar gharana (1884-1953). Aman Ali Khan had the same Carnatic inflection in his singing style that distinguished Abdul Karim Khan. He was a gifted composer. He was well known for his khayal compositions in Hamsadhwani, the khayals *'Lagi lagan'* and *'Jai math vilamba'*. The Khan saheb specialised in the Merukhand approach to the scales which, for his time, was rather unusual.

Amir Khan (1912-1974) was a master of the Indore gharana whose other well-known representative is Pandit Amarnath. The microscopic detailed approach to the raga's vistar was a characteristic of his style. His taans had a very special geometrical quality derived from the Merukhand approach to scales. He had also developed a special style of tarana.

Amir Khusro (1253-1325) was a legendary poet and musician. He was court poet to eleven emperors including Alauddin Khilji. Hazrat Nizamuddin Auliya was the guru of Amir Khusro and he belonged to the Qawwal Bacche tradition, whose contribution to Hindustani music has been varied and deep. Khusro was a poet besides being a musician, whose compositions in Brij bhasha are widely acclaimed. He is believed to be the father of the present khayal form and of the qawwali, and of instruments like the sitar and the dholak. The Tala Sulfakta is also known to have been devised by him.

anahata is the sound (nada) that is not heard except in the heart. It is the yogic awareness of a primal vibration. It is the opposite of ahata nada which is the heard sound. (See also AHATA.)

anakshara alap is alap that has no words or syllables or mnemonics conveying verbal meanings. Its opposite is sakshara alap.

Ananda Bhairav is a raga in the Hindustani music tradition and belongs to the Bhairav thaat. It is a morning raga.

Ananda Bhairavi is a Carnatic raga of the twentieth melakarta, Natabhairavi. Syama Shastri's '*O Jagadamba*' is widely popular. It is not found in Hindustani music although the Maharashtra stage song beginning '*Dehata sharangata*' from the play *Manapaman* is supposed to be an imitation of the Carnatic Ananda Bhairavi. It is sung as a mixture of the ragas Kafi and Pilu.

Anandi also called Ananda Kalyan or merely Nand is a popular raga of Hindustani music. It belongs to the Kalyan thaat and is a shadava-sampoorna raga. There is no raga in Carnatic music by this name or with similar traits. However there are several film songs composed in the south based on this raga. A popular bandish in this raga is '*Aja hoon na aye shyam*'.

andola(m) is one of the ten gamakas mentioned in the *Sangeeta Makaranda*. It is a grace and consists of a long amplitude vibrato that bends the note in relatively quick succession but not fast enough to make the sound feel like vibrato. It produces a kind of stress and emotional quality in the raga's note. (See GAMAKA.)

anga literally means a limb or a part. In music it refers to a style such as raga anga, thumri anga and tappa anga. The anga in raga anga would be used to indicate the root to which a given raga might belong. Anga also refers to the two tetrachords—the lower or the poorvang and the upper or the uttarang. It could also denote one of the divisions of musical time. There are six angas—dhruta, anudruta, guru, laghu, pluta, and kaka pada.

angulastana is the finger-board of a musical instrument.

angusattoni is a well-known printer's devil that is reputed to have been made in the first edition of *Nandanar Charitram* for the raga Hamsadhwani.

anibaddha is one of the two types of music—the NIBADDHA and the anibaddha variety. Unlike the nibaddha, the anibaddha does not have a tala structure or any noticeable intended design.

aniloma is the term used to describe singing or playing a theme at various degrees of speed, while keeping the basic tala unchanged. This means the kriti is first sung once at its basic speed, then twice at double its speed, and at double that or four times the basic speed in the third stage.

antara is the second movement of a bandish or a rachana. It is usually composed for the uttarang, or the upper tetrachord of a raga. (See DHATU.) Antara also denotes the swara gandhara of the musical scale in its vikrut characteristic as described by Bharata.

antara gandhara is the higher of the sharp *E* of the European scale or the *Mi* interval of the solfege. This is the fifth harmonic note with a frequency of 5/4. The Hindustani system does not name this position of the note. It is left to the ears of the singer to position the note.

antara marga is among the thirteen lakshanas or associated characteristics of the nature of a raga. This consists in introducing a swara into a raga which is foreign to it and therefore prohibited. But despite such a violation of rule, the effect of this attempt does not violate the basic design and feeling of the raga but adds to its piquancy and inner values. Ordinarily this is a difficult thing to do and cannot be done in all ragas.

anubandha is the final and concluding section of a composition. It functions much like a coda of a sonata in European music. Anubandha gives a composition a kind of finality. The practice of singing the anubandha has become less prevalent in recent times. There are several kritis in Carnatic music that have anubandha sections. The kriti *'Viri Boni'* in Raga Bhairavi and Thyagaraja's Pancharatna *'Sadhincheve'* in Raga Arabhi have anubandhas.

anudatta is the name given to the lowest note in the Rig Vedic chant that has three notes in its scale. The two other notes are called udatta and swarita. (See ADI SWARA.)

anudruta (anudrutam) is one of the six ANGAS used in the measure of musical time. Its duration is one akshara kala and is a relative measure.

anumandra is the region of the scale that lies below the shadja in the kharaj space of the scale. Normally voices do not go that low and this region is used only in instrumental music. The *basso profondo* in Western music is the male voice that sometimes goes even beyond the anumandra.

anunada is the name given to the hushed gandhara that is heard when the mandra string of a tanpura is tuned to the bass tonic. This gandhara is the fifth harmonic note. It is also called the swayambhu gandhara.

(See also SWAYAMBHU.)

anupallavi is the second movement of a kriti or a varnam padam in Carnatic music. It is the equivalent of the antara in a Hindustani bandish. Its length could be either the same as the pallavi or twice its length.

anusarani means the secondary string. It is the second of the two middle strings of the tanpura which are tuned to the tonic note or the shadja swara. When the sarani, which is the string closest to the panchama string of the tanpura, and the anusarani are perfectly tuned, if one of them is plucked, the other vibrates sympathetically.

anuswara is the third note heard as an echo of the basic sound in a tanpura's bass note or its kharaj shadja. This sound enriches the tuning of the tanpura and has a quality of beauty that is difficult to match in any other instrument.

anuvadi is the note which is neither the VADI nor the SAMVADI of a raga and therefore is neither a perfect fifth nor fourth. It is not the VIVADI or taboo swara either. All ragas have two pivotal swaras called vadi and samvadi while the other swaras are neither. These are called the anuvadi swaras.

apaswara is a swara whose pitch has poor focus. It is a false note or a note that is off-key. Besura also means the same. It has a jarring effect on the ears.

apoorna means incomplete. It is a raga which is not SAMPOORNA in its ascending and descending scale.

Arabhi is a janya raga that is derived from the twenty-ninth melakarta, Dheera Shankarabharanam.

arangetram is the first

performance given by a singer or a player, a dancer or an actor after his/her period of training, before an invited audience. It is often done in a temple before a deity as an offering to God.

archika means singing to one note. This is often indicated for certain passages of the Rig Veda where the recitation should be in one note.

aroha (**arohana**) is a series of notes in the ascending order of pitch. Arohanatwa is the ascending state of a raga in alap, where its scale is still to ascend and explore the upper reaches of the raga scale.

arohana-avarohana is commonly used to describe the ascending and descending order of notes of a raga, the barest skeleton of its structure. (See also AVAROHANA.)

arya is a verse in the Kathakalakshepam of South India, usually sung in a loose rhythm. It is structured in the Arya metre and most often the raga in which it is sung is Bihag.

Asavari is a popular raga of the Hindustani tradition, belonging to the Asavari thaat. In the Carnatic tradition, it belongs in the twentieth melakarta Natabhairavi.

Asaveri is a Carnatic raga from the eighth melakarta, Hanumatodi.

ashtapadi literally means eight verses and is the name given to the well-known poetry of Jayadeva in the *Gita Govinda*. In this work there are twenty-six ashtapadis.

ati komal literally means very flat, ordinarily one shruti lower than the standard komal position of a note. (See KOMAL.)

ati tara saptak is the octave above the TARA SAP-

TAK. It is the third octave above the middle octave.

Atrauli gharana (See JAIPUR GHARANA.)

audava literally means five, meaning five notes.

audava-audava is a raga that has five notes each in ascent and descent. Ragas like Durga, Hamsadhwani and Bhoopali are audava-audava ragas.

audava-sampoorna raga is a raga that has only five notes in its ascent but has all seven notes in its descent. Bhimpalasi in the Hindustani tradition is an audava-sampoorna raga.

avarohana (avarohi) is the descending scale of notes of a raga. (See AROHANA.)

avarta (avartanam) represents the passage of a lyric through one cycle of the tala from its first matra to its last. One cycle is completed when the tala cycle returns to its first position.

B

B is the seventh note of the European major scale. It is the nishad of the Indian scale or the interval *Ni* and thus is the *Ti* of the solfege.

babat is the clear configuration of the swaras of a raga that reveals the principal and unambiguous character of the raga.

bada khayal indicates the older or the larger musical composition. This is a slow-moving piece of music sung in vilambit laya which is slower than the walking pace of the andante and falls into something between the allegretto and adagio. The vilambit of the khayal is slow, half or a quarter or even an eighth of what is called medium tempo in Hindustani music.

Badari is a janya raga of the twenty-sixth melakarta, Charukesi. It could also indicate the leather thongs that bind the top percussive section of the tabla to its sides, and fixes the top securely. It is always made from the hides of dead animals such as pigs.

Badarika is a janya raga derived from the fifty-first melakarta, Kamavardhini.

badhat means an orderly development of musical ideas in a raga in the form of alap.

Bagesari Bahar is a janya raga of Hindustani music derived from the ninth melakarta, Dhenuka.

Bagesari is a Hindustani raga corresponding to the Carnatic Sriranjani.

Bagesri is a very popular raga of the night in Hindustani music. It belongs in the Kafi thaat. There are three types of Bagesri—audava-shadava, shadava-shadava, and shadava-sampoorna. The bandish *'Kaun gata bhayee'* is very popular. In Carnatic music there is no raga called Bagesri. Vageeshwari of Carnatic music is a janya of the melakarta Kankanangi, which is the first melakarta.

Bahaduri Todi belongs in the Todi thaat. It is a shadava-shadava raga of the morning. There is no raga called Bahaduri Todi in Carnatic music. The raga Shekharachandrika, which is the forty-fifth melakarta, has the same scale as Bahaduri Todi.

bahao means an easy fluency of gait of musical ideas.

Bahar is a very popular Hindustani raga. Literally, bahar means spring. This raga belongs in the Kafi thaat which is the Karaharapriya of the south. It is sung at night and is a shadava-sampoorna raga. The bandish *'Nai ritu nai phooli'* in this raga is very popular. There is no raga called Bahar in Carnatic music. The Southern Kanada, which belongs in the Karaharapriya melakarta, resembles Bahar.

Bahattara Melakarta is the text in Marathi composed by the famous Tanjore poet, Lavani Venkata Rao. The 72 melakartas contained in this book indicate all the raga mudras, or the distinguishing fingerprints of a raga. It is also called the KANAKANGIRATNANGI nomenclature. Sakharam Saheb wanted the Marathi sahitya of this book put to music and asked Mahavaidyanatha Iyer to do this. This was completed and a concert of this music was performed in 1883.

Bahudamani is a janya raga of the fifty-first mela, Kamavardhini.

Bahudamari is a janya raga of the twenty-eighth melakarta, Hari Kambhoji. Thyagaraja's *'Brova bharama'* is a popular kriti in this raga.

Bahudari in Carnatic music, is a janya of the twenty-eighth melakarta, Harikambhoji, which corresponds to the Hindustani Khamaj and is a shadava-audava raga. The Thyagaraja composition *'Brova bharama'* is popular. The Hindustani Raga Tilang comes closest to the Carnatic Bahudari.

bahutwa is the trayodasa lakshana of a raga or its thirteen characteristics. It is related to those prayogas that can be used many times without diminution of meaning. There are two varieties of bahutwa—the abhyasa bahutwa, which is a group of notes that can be used repeatedly; and the alanghana bahutwa, which is a note that can be used with premeditation and care and then stressed appropriately.

Baiju Bawara (1486-1526) also known as Naik Baiju and Baijnath Mishra, was a celebrated dhrupad singer at the court of Man Singh Tomar of Gwalior and had a reputation equalling that of Tansen's.

baj is a characteristic style of playing a plucked instrument such as the sitar, the sarod, the veena, or percussion instruments like the tabla and the pakhawaj. Tones that are sustained as in wind instruments or bowed ones do not admit to recognition as baj. In sitar, for instance, there are two principal baj—masitkhani and razakhai. There is no baj in sarangi, which is bowed, or the shehnai or flute, which are both blown through.

baj ka tar is the string of an instrument in which the principal melody is played.

Bakshu Naik was a

famous singer in the Gwalior court during the early sixteenth century.

bakura is a wind instrument mentioned in the Rig Veda.

bala is the name of the third shruti or microtone of panchama in Narada's nomenclature of twenty-two shrutis. (See SANGEETA MAKARANDA and SHRUTI.)

Balabi is a raga derived from the fifty-fourth melakarta, Vishwambari.

Balahari is a janya raga derived from the twenty-ninth melakarta, Dhira Shankarabharanam.

balasaraswati is also called the mayuri veena. It is a North Indian instrument, its resonator shaped and coloured like a peacock. It is played like a cello with the neck on the shoulder and the peacock's feet on the ground. It has many sympathetic strings and is played with a bow.

Jaganatha Bhatgoswami used to be a well-known player of the balasaraswati and was much admired in the Tanjore court. This instrument is not in use any longer.

Balaswami Dikshitar (1786–1858) was the youngest brother of the great composer Muthuswami. He was a genius of his time. He engaged a European violinist to teach him to play the violin and he studied the instrument assiduously for three years. Balaswami Dikshitar was the first to adopt the violin to play Carnatic music. He could also play the veena and the sitar. He made the JUGALBANDI popular. It came to be known as jodi pattu in the south. He sang with his brother, Chinnaswami, at concerts which became widely acclaimed.

Bana is the name of the fifth chakra among the twelve chakras into which the melakartas have been divided. Each chakra has six mela ragas. The name of the fifth chakra is Bana in the system of 72 melakartas, comprising the melas 25–50.

bandish is a composition that is defined as bound. These are normally composed in Brij bhasha or Bhojpuri or other dialects of the Hindi heartland where space is provided for musical elaboration through a felicitous selection of vowel sounds. A poem in this sense is not a bandish even if it can be bound by tala, for its structure is complete in itself and does not need musical elaboration for enrichment. Poets do not compose bandishes, musicians do. The instrumental compositions of GATS are also loosely called bandish.

banee is the resonance of the sayings of saints. The phrase 'Come unto me all who suffer and hunger after righteousness' would qualify as banee in this context. The Sikh Gurbani is one such. This word is somewhat extended when it is used to refer to dhrupad styles of singing such as Khandahar banee, Dagar banee, and so on. A banee is beyond the meaning of the words that describe it. The sayings of the saints, for example, have to be understood psychologically.

Bangala Varala is the raga in which the twenty-fifth Ashtapadi of Jayadeva is composed.

Bangali is a raga mentioned in the *Sangeeta Ratnakara* and the *Sangeeta Makaranda*.

banka is a wind instrument commonly used as an accompaniment at temple festivals. Classical music is also played on these instruments.

bansuri is the flute used in Hindustani classical music.

bant describes the divisions or apportioning of words, swara and laya in a musical expression. In a dhrupad, when a singer sings a line or a word in more than one way, it is often called a swara bant. When the variation is achieved in rhythm it is called laya bant.

barahmasa means twelve months. The term is used to describe the folk traditions of Uttar Pradesh. They describe the life of common people. They are sung in classical ragas and describe each of the twelve months of the year.

Barbara is a janya raga derived from the sixty-fourth melakarta, Vachaspati.

barhat is a kind of sarod-like instrument made of wood, with a few frets, used in folk music.

bari is the longer variety of nagaswaram, a wind instrument, as contrasted with the shorter variety called timiri. The bari has a lower pitch when compared to the timiri. (See NAGASWARAM.)

Barkat Ali was the younger brother of the doyen of Patiala, Bade Gulam Ali Khan. After the partition of India Barkat Ali remained in Pakistan. He was a thumri and ghazal singer of protean power. Begum Akhtar and most of the great thumri and ghazal singers of this age owe to him their appeal and power.

Basant distantly resembles Raga Vasanta in Carnatic music. Basant in the Hindustani tradition belongs in the Poorvi thaat and in Carnatic music, Vasanta derives from the sixteenth melakarta, Mayamalavagaula. In the Hindustani system, Basant is sung in spring.

bass bar is a piece of wood which is attached to the underside of bowed instruments like the viola, the violin, the cello, and the double-bass. It supports the pressure on the bridge of the violin and smoothes out the notes, distributing the vibrations of the strings equally.

bastran is a Burmese instrument. It has a boat-shaped resonating base on which twenty-one pieces of wood of different sizes are laid out. When struck they produce twenty-one different notes of the scale.

baul refers to the ecstatic, possessed state of the singers of this genre. Those who sing these type of songs are also called baul. It is also the term for a kind of devotional music of Bengal, which is said to produce this ecstatic state.

Bauli is a janya raga derived from the fifteenth melakarta, Mayamalava-gaula.

bayalata is the Kannada yakshagana or open-air play.

bayan constitutes the left half of the pair of drums called tabla.

been is a seven-stringed instrument with frets and two large resonators. The instrument is held oblique-ly, the left resonator rest-ing on the shoulder of the player. The instrument has a solemn sepulchral tone, deep and mysterious. Assad Ali Khan is a contemporary master of this instrument in Hindustani music.

beenkar is a player of the been.

been-sitar is a veena of the been class but whose frets can be moved and ad-justed, while in the been they are fixed.

Begada is a janya raga from the twenty-ninth melakarta, Dhira Shank-arabharanam.

Begum Akhtar (1914-1974) was the name by which Akhtari Bai Faizabadi was popularly known. She had among the most appealing voices in light music. She was one of the foremost exponents of what is called the Poorab ang thumri. She mixed the Punjabi with the Poorab ang so deftly that it emerged as a unique style of her own. She acknowledged Abdul Wahid Khan of Kirana, Barkat Ali of Patiala and Ramzan Khan of Lucknow as her gurus. She has several students whom she has influenced with her art.

behla is the Indian equivalent for the word violin. It could also be a corruption of the word viola.

behlava is the use of the words of the composition that is being sung in the alap to explicate meaning and mood.

behr is the metrical structure of poetry.

beroza is the sticky honey-coloured resin that is the residue after the distillation of crude turpentine. This is used to rub the horsehair of the bow of a violin or a viola or cello to raise the vibrancy and loudness of the sound of the bowed instrument. It is also called rosin.

besura means apaswara or out of tune.

betaal is music that is out of rhythm, missing beats.

bhaand is a group of minstrels, clowns and jesters who use music in their art. The bhaand are mostly found in Punjab and Uttar Pradesh.

bhaat is a tribe of Rajput singers who sung of the chivalry and heraldic traditions of Rajput kings and their exploits on the battlefield.

Bhadrachala is the signature a seventeenth century poet and musician, Bhadrachala Ramadasa, used in his compositions.

Bhadrachalam is a place situated on the northern

bank of the Godavari river on the eastern border of Andhra Pradesh. It is a place hallowed by the memory of Saint Bhadrachala Ramadasa.

Bhadragandhari is a raga derived from the twenty-ninth melakarta, Dhira Shankarabharanam.

Bhadrakali pattu are songs related to the deity Bhadrakali in Malabar temples.

bhagavata bhajana paddhati is an impressive anthology of sacred songs which include selections from Marathi, Telugu, Kannada and Sanskrit composers. These have been compiled in sequential order in the *Bhagavata Bhajanotsava Paddhati*.

bhagavata goshti consists of a group of singers singing sacred songs in South India

bhagavata mela natakam are the devotional dance and song performances in the presence of temple deities during the annual temple festivals.

bhagavatar is the name given to the performers of KATHAKALAKSHEPAM or religious discourses to the accompaniment of music.

Bhairava literally means the fearsome sounding one. It was the name given to the devotees of Shiva who are said to have lived in cremation grounds. The men were called Bhairava and the women were called Bhairavi. The raga has been called Bhairavi. This is the scale corresponding to the scale of Mayamalavagaula in the Carnatic tradition. Bhairavi can be compared to the Carnatic Todi raga.

bhajan is any tune that has a devotional quality, whose words are adorative of deities and tell of the myths associated with them. Mira, Tulsidas and Kabir are the principal bhajan composers whose lyrics are sung in Hindustani music.

bhakt is the devoted one in the musical sense as well as in the religious sense.

bharana is the concept associated with the practice of the swara of scales. The idea is to think of the swara as though it was a being filled with voice so that the swara seems like a process of filling.

Bharata is the illustrious author of the Sanskrit text, *Natya Shastra*, the most ancient treatise dealing with the science of dramaturgy and music. It is a text written in the fourth century BC. The name Bharata is also believed to be an acronym of the words 'bhava', 'raga' and 'tala'.

Bharati, Gopalakrishna (1810-1896) is a name revered as much as Thyagaraja. Among Tamil composers he is the greatest. Some of his com-

positions in rare ragas became very popular. These include 'Sivalokame' in Raga Natakapriya, 'Sivakamasundari' in Jaganmohini and the famous Mauji raga 'Jalapadavendum'. He also developed folk forms like lavani and cheendu into striking musical forms.

bhasha is one of the Margi ragas of which there are six in ancient music. Sarangadeva mentions them in his famous *Sangita Ratnakara*.

Bhaskar Bua Bhakhle (1869-1922) was among the acknowledged masters of music of his time. His teachers were Ustad Alladiya Khan of Jaipur and Ustad Nathan Khan of Agra. He trained Dileep Chand Vedi, Bhai Lal and Master Krishna, who also acted and sang in films.

Bhatkhande, Vishnu Narayan (1860–1936) was among the greatest of contemporary musicologists and could be said to have launched Indian classical music in its journey into the modern era. He had been trained in music as a child. He also took a degree in law and began practising it. His first love, however, was music, and over the years he began to devote most of his time to music and its study. He designed an effective notation and travelled all over India collecting bandishes from a wide variety of gharanas and styles. This finally became the volumes one to four of the Marathi language collection called *Hindustani Sangeet Padhati*. Later he put together six volumes in Hindi of the series called *Hindustani Sangeet Padhati Kramik Pusthak* which has become the single most important source book of Hindustani classical music. He convened the first All India Music Conference in Baroda in 1916 and followed it up with regular conferences in other cities

of the north. He trained several musicians in his time, the most well-known among them being Shri Krishna Narayan Ratanjankar, who later became the principal of the Bhathkhande college of music in Lucknow.

Several institutions came up in Bhatkhande's name —the Khairagarh, the Lucknow Bhatkhande College of Music, the Bhatkhande Sangeet Vidyapeeth and the Madhav Music University at Gwalior. The system of Hindustani music notation that he evolved has become the standard observed all over North India for nearly two generations and has become the basis of all music notations in this tradition.

He introduced the janakajanya system of raga classification in Hindustani classical music. From the seventy-two melakartas of Carnatic music he chose ten crucial ones and called them thaats. This was a kind of periodic table for ragas which was the current technique of classification in the Carnatic system. The correspondences he arrived at were:

The thaat Bhairavi corresponds to the eighth mela, Hanumatodi of the Carnatic classification. Bhairav corresponds to the fifteenth mela, Mayamalavagaula. The Asavari thaat corresponds to the twentieth melakarta, Nathabhairavi and the Kafi thaat corresponds to the twenty-second melakarta Karaharapriya. Khamaj thaat corresponds to the twenty-eighth melakarta Harikambhoji and the Bilawal thaat corresponds to the twenty-ninth melakarta, Dhira Shankarabharanam. The Todi thaat corresponds to the forty-fifth melakarta Subhapantuvarali, and the Poorvi thaat corresponds to the fifty-first melakarta, Kamavardhini. The Marwa thaat corresponds to the fifty-third mela, Gaman srama and the Yeman thaat corresponds to the sixty-fifth melakarta, Mechakalyani. The following works of Bhatkhande are seminal and constitute the basis of much of the written material on contemporary Hindustani music: *A Short Historical Survey of the Music of Upper India*; *A Comparative Study of Some of the Leading Music Systems of the 15th, 16th, 17th and 18th Centuries*; *Hindustani Sangeet Paddhati* (Marathi and Hindi) in 7 volumes; *Abhinava Raga Manjari* and *Shrimallakshya Sangit*. The last two of these books were written under the pen name Vishnu Sharma.

bhava is the soul of the raga, the emotional bed which gives life to the scale of a raga. Without bhava a raga is a mere scale. The ability to fill a scale with bhava is the secret of genius in raga music. The restraint and economy and the tension that bhavas produce is the foundation of a musician's art. Sadhana in music is principally directed towards the production of bhava.

Bhendi Bazar gharana started with the Bijnor brothers who were singers settled in the Bhendi Bazar area of Bombay. There were three of them—Chajju Khan, Nazir Khan, and Khadim Husein Khan. Chajju became a faqir (mystic). He wrote under the pseudonym Amar Muni and his compositions had a spiritual content. Ustad Chajju Khan's son Aman Ali Khan became a major exponent of the gharana. A large number of the compositions of this gharana are in praise of Lord Shiva. Shiv Kumar Shukla and Ramesh Nadkarni were famous pupils of this gharana and its major voice was that of Anjanibai Malpeker.

bheree is a bugle used in the time of war and also in reveille. Classical music can be played on this instrument.

Bhimpalasi is a raga which is a combination of Bhim and Palasi. It is a popular raga in Hindustani music and is sung early in the evening. It belongs to the Kafi thaat (Karaharapriya melakarta) and is an audava-sampoorna raga.

Bhoopali is a raga belonging to the Kalyan thaat, which is Mechakalyani in the Carnatic tradition. It is an audava-audava raga.

bhriga (birka) is a musical phrase of great beauty and allure in Hindustani music. This is also called a **khatka**.

Bijnor brothers (See BHENDI BAZAR GHARANA.)

Bilas Khan was the famous son of Mian Tansen. Bilas Khan was the first to sing the raga, Bilaskhani Todi. He is said to have sung it at the feet of the dead Tansen. The body of Tansen is said to have blessed him at the end of the rendition. Thereafter Bilas Khan was called a Khaleefa, or an Emperor of the Tansen inheritance.

Bilaskhani Todi is the raga discovered by Tansen's son Bilas Khan. It corresponds to the Carnatic Suddha Todi.

Bilawal thaat is the scale in Hindustani music that corresponds to the twenty-ninth melakarta, Dhira Shankarabharanam, in Carnatic music.

Binkar is the name given to the descendants of Naubat Khan, the son-in-law of Mian Tansen. The descendents along Tansen's son, Bilas Khan's line, are known as RABABIYYAS. They play the rabab.

biradai is a Tamil word meaning the tuning peg of a stringed instrument. The Tanjore tanpuras have a square peg like the violin. Others have round knobs.

birka See BHRIGA.

biruda is one of the six angas or movements of the PRABANDHA and usually consists of a phrase of praise for the nayaka (actor, protagonist).

bol literally means a phrase of music in words or mnemonics with the rhythmic solfa syllables of tala like *dha dhin dha*. In Carnatic music this is referred to as **jati** or **solkattu**.

bol banao refers to the composition of a new phrase while singing ragas to enhance the acuity of meaning.

bol bant is the division of phrases to accentuate meaning. It is an essential feature of dhrupad singing and can also be seen in the khayals built on the dhrupad anga.

bol taan consists of the musical figures that are produced when the words of a bandish are used to elaborate the geometries of swaras and words in brand new figures. These are at their best in madhyalaya and use the style of the tala to enhance the beauty of their gait.

bow is a stick strung with horsehair that is used to play bowed instruments like the sarangi and the violin.

Brahma is the name of the ninth chakra in the 72 melakarta scheme comprising melas 49-54. There are 12 chakras with 6 ragas each in the 72 melakarta scheme. Brahma is the ninth chakra.

brahma vina is regarded as a kind of tanpura used to accompany Hindustani music. It is also referred to simply as a vina and is described in works such as the *Sangita Makaranda*, *Narada Sangita Sudhakara* of Hari Pala Deva (fourteenth century) and the *Sangita Parijata* of Ahobala. The brahma vina has 24 houses or inner spaces for its frets. The structure of the modern vina, in fact, is the same.

bridge is the piece of wood in a stringed instrument over which the strings are stretched.

Brihaddesi is a seminal work of the fifth century by Matanga Muni. The jatis of the time of Bharata had become dormant in Matanga's time and ragas had taken their place. The *Brihaddesi* gives a lucid account of raga classification, such as suddha, chhayalaga, sankirna and so on. There is also a section on nadotpatti or the origin of nada, shruti, swara murchhana, varna, alankara, giti, jati, raga, bhasha, prabandha etc. It is also said to have had a chapter on musical instruments which is now lost. The Trivandrum Sanskrit Series publication omits this chapter. That later writers have held the chapter on vadyadhyaya of the *Brihaddesi* in high regard shows that Matanga was an authority on the subject.

Brihaspathi is the name of the sage who was an authority on music.

bulbul taranga is a stringed instrument with a typewriter kind of keyboard. It was invented by the Japanese. It was considered an instrument to be used as a toy by those who enjoyed playing random music.

bundle flute is a reed dulcimer consisting of a sheaf of pan flutes.

Bundu Khan (1886–1955) was a well known sarangi player of the Delhi gharana. A disciple of Mamman Khan who was a member of the Patiala royal court, Bundu Khan became a court musician at Indore. Bundu Khan changed the catgut string for a metal one in the sarangi. His son was Umrao Khan, a singer as well as a sarangi player. He lived in Pakistan.

C

C is the first note of the European Major scale.

castanets are usually two pieces of rosewood or ivory held in each hand and struck together to play the rhythm of a piece of music. It is also called the CHIPLA and is often used by Kathakalakshepam and bhajan singers who sing congregationally.

chachar is the name given to the tala Deepchandi played with thumris or other light forms of music. Its bol is *dhin dhin-dha dha-tin tin-ta ta-tin tin-dha dha-dhin dhin*, making fourteen beats in all.

chachhari is a kind of musical composition built like the PRABANDHA and is referred to in the *Sangeeta Sudha* and consists of three movements, long, stately in gait and slow to expound.

Chaitanya (1485-1534) was a major saint of the Bhakti movement in Bengal and Orissa. He was a devotee of Lord Krishna and sang in a state of ecstasy and abandon. He composed many hundred devotional songs that aro sung to this day by those who follow Chaitanya Prabhu's teachings on love and God's spirit.

chaiti are songs that relate to the leelas of Krishna and Radha and are sung in the month of chaitra (March-April). This music belongs to northern Uttar Pradesh. The words of this music are in Brij bhasha or what is called Purabia. This music is also popular in Bihar. Light ragas like Pahadi, Mand and Asa are used in the chaitis, as also Pilu and Kouncilia.

chakkar is a circle or a ring of the tala's cycle whether in tala itself or in taans. It is a circular motion of notes, whether illustrated through tala cycles or not.

chakkardar is a series of cycles of taans or talas.

chakra is a configuration or a scheme of organisation, for example, the ten thaats of Hindustani music or the seventy-two melakartas of Carnatic music. In melakarta arrangements there are twelve chakras and each chakra has six ragas making seventy-two melas in all.

chakra bandhana are a whole set of arpeggios or fast alankaras and swara geometries on the veena which are played within the tight compass of five or six frets. The fingers of the left hand can be seen touching all of the four strings of the veena at the same time, or successively at rapid speed, producing momentary harmonic colour.

chakradhar consists of any set of taans or toda or tukda which returns to the sam after three or more rounds through the avartas.

chakra taan is one of the six kinds of taans. Like rotating wheels the notes whirl round and round at great speed. Most singers are unable to sing these varieties of taans so they are not often heard.

Chakravakam is the sixteenth melakarta raga. Thyagaraja made this raga popular with his kriti.

chalan is the characteristic gait of a raga which is the key to identifying it. The word *chaal* is its root. It is an identifiable manner of movement in the raga.

Chalanta is the name of the thirty-sixth melakarta. This is a raga which is not commonly heard.

chanchar is a fourteen

matra tala divided into four sections of alternating three and four units. The first, the fourth, and the eleventh matras have beats and the eighth is khali or empty.

chantee is the leather membrane made from animal skin which con-stitutes the taut striking face of the dayan (right-hand piece) of the tabla. The mnemonics or bols played on the tabla are called **chantee ke bol**.

Chanterelle is the highest pitched string of any stringed instrument—veena, guitar, violin, cello, sitar or sarod and so on. The *E* string is the first string on the violin. Most instruments tune the first string to the highest pitch. In the veena this string is closest to the player while in the sitar and rudra veena it is at the opposite end.

chara veena is a portable veena, unlike the **sthira**

veena which used to be kept in an open place and worked as an aeolian harp which was sounded when the wind blew through its strings.

Charan Rajput(s) are minstrels who sing songs of heroism and recite poetry of valour and sacrifice and victory.

charanam is the third part of any composition or kriti in the Carnatic tradi-tion.

Charju is a famed musician who is supposed to have composed the raga, Charju Malhar.

Charukesi is a raga of the thirty-sixth melakarta.

Chatura Kallinatha is the author of the commen-tary named *Kalanidhi* on the *Sangeeta Ratnakara*.

Chatur Pandit is the *nom de plume* of Pandit Vishnu Narayan Bhat-khande. (See BHAT-KHANDE.)

chaturang denotes four sections. 'Chatur' denotes four and 'ang' denotes parts or sections or limbs. It is descriptive of the four parts of music—khayal, tarana, sargam and tirwat. A khayal is a composition also called a bandish. It may have two or three movements and is usually composed in Brij bhasha. The tarana is a mnemonically structured composition whose syllables *ta da tere* and other similar mnemonics are built in the same way as a khayal composed of two movements. The sargam are solfege syllables put to tala. They may also be free, open-ended phrases that are part of the elaboration of a raga. Tirwat is a composition that has three sections consisting of sargams, tabla bols and tarana.

chaturasra laghu is the variety of laghu that consists of a beat that is followed by three finger counts, thus making for four aksharakalas.

Chaturdanda Praka-shika is Venkatmukhi's famous book written about the year 1635. The title of the book, when translated, would mean an exposition of the CHATURDANDI or the four distinct ways in which a raga can be born. The book is in Sanskrit and handles subjects like veena, shruti, swara, mela, raga, alap, laya, prabandha, geetaprabandha and so on. The melakarta organisation is discussed at length in this book. Venkatmukhi uses the seven notes of the musical scale and their twelve variations as the basis for the 72 melakarta classification. The nineteen main melas and the fifty-five ragas born from them are described at length. This organisation of seventy-two melakartas is a remarkable arrangement of scales and belongs in a class by itself. Venkatmukhi does not attempt to give the system any nomenclature. He merely leaves them classified in seventy-two scales. The later Kanakangi nomenclature kept the mela and the raga apart. This began to be used not earlier than 1735.

chaturdandi is defined as the four means of expressing the essence of a raga—geeta, alapana, laya and prabandha. This definition was given in King Talaja's *Sangita Saramrita*. There is another explanation of chaturdandi also extant which describes it as four sections such as the sthayi, aroha, avaroha and sanchari.

chaturdasa murcchanas are the fourteen murcchanas or scales that are born out of what is known as grama bheda, that is the process of shifting the tonic to successive notes of any scale. This modal shift is obtained by shifting from the sa grama and the ma grama. The sa grama

means the shift that first establishes the scale taken from the *sa,* then shifting to each of the remaining notes, to *ni* and *dha* and *pa ma ga re sa.* The madhyama grama begins with *ma* as the tonic and then moves to *ga ri sa ni dha* and *pa* as tonics successively.

chaturtha jati is a kind of taan which uses four notes in a single cluster as it moves.

chatusruti rishabha is the higher or teevra rishabha whose frequency is 9/8. It is a term used in Carnatic music.

chautal is a tala of seventy-two beats or matras usually used in dhruvapad (dhrupad). Its twelve matras are divided into six sections in which the first matra is the sam, the third and the seventh are khalis, with a beat each on the fifth and the eleventh.

cheez is used to refer to a khayal composition. It is an Urdu word and literally means a thing.

chempata is the term for Adi tala in Kathakali music.

chenda is a drum shaped like a cylinder used in Kerala's Kathakali dance. A solo performance on the chenda is usually the opening of a Kathakali performance. Its talas are the same as in classical music.

chhand is the rhythmic structure of a lyric whose metres match.

chhayalaga raga is a raga that has minute traces of another raga in its exposition, which are not clear but smudged and uncertain.

chhoot is a fast taan that shoots across the scale leaving out some notes along the way.

chhota khayal is a kind of bandish which, unlike the vilambit khayal, has a tightness of phrase and structure. Its gait is swift (madhya and dhrut) and its design has figures that extol the laya of the bandish. It is a natural growing of the raga from the vilambit khayal to the chhota khayal as a further elaboration and exploration of the raga and its possibilities. There are differences of opinion about the chhota khayal's origin. There are many who consider Hazrat Amir Khusro to be the first to compose chhota khayals. Others attribute this to the Jaipur Sultan Husein Sharki, some to Raj Bahadur and Chanchal Sen.

chhoot taan is a phrase in which two or more swaras are omitted in the fast passage of the phrase.

chikari are two strings, one tuned to the middle octave shadja and the other to the upper octave shadja in sitars, surbahar and other string instruments. They are found at the end of a set of strings on which the tune is played. These are the strings that are played in the JHALA sequence of a performance. Its sound effect is that of a distant ghungroo.

chilla is a voluntary discipline with spiritual and transformative effects. A musician isolates himself and practises his art in seclusion. Usually this isolation in ritual terms lasts forty (chilla) days but is practised for varying periods by those who enter the world of music with all their strength and life. This vow is taken before a pir in a graveyard or before the mazhar of a Muslim saint. It is a custom in the Hindustani music tradition. The impact of such a retreat on a musician is sometimes miraculous, making him manifest a strange and haunting quality in his art.

chipla is a pair of castanets used by bhagavatars for keeping rhythm during their performances.

Chishti is a musical inheritance or parampara that originated from the Khwaja Moinuddin Chishti Garib Nawaz (1142-1235), the Sufi saint who settled in Ajmer. He had several disciples, the most notable among them being Bakhtiar Kaki and his disciple, Sheikh Farid. Among the line of Sufi saints included in the Chishti tradition is Nizamuddin Auliya (1238-1325), whose famous disciple was Amir Khusro. The khayal and qawwali were born from this tradition.

chitra veena is a type of stringed instrument with seven strings.

chitta swara(s) are a series of set swara-geometries usually sung at the end of a kriti for its sonorous appeal. It comes after the anupallavi and the charanam in Carnatic music. It is usually sung at the same speed as the rest of the composition. These swaras are usually composed by the composer of the kriti himself though there have been instances when chitta swaras were added on by someone else for some kritis.

chyuta shadja is the note slightly higher than the kakali nishada and lies between the kakali nishada and the tara shadja. Its frequency is the Pythagorean seventh. In the raga Kurunji this chyuta shadja is used.

chyuta shadja-nishada See CHYUTA SHADJA.

clarinet is a wood-wind instrument with a two-and-a-half octave range. It is cylindrical in shape and has a single reed with keys. It is used in Carnatic music orchestras.

counterpoint is the simultaneous playing of two or more melodies each of which has musical significance independent of each other. One is deemed to be the counterpoint of the other. It is possible to have several melodies running together, triple and quadruple counterpoint, which can take up any position with respect to each other.

cycle of five are the panchama swaras of any given shadja, in the same way as the cycle of fourths is the madhyama of each given shadja. A simple example is to take a shadja. Its fifth note will be panchama and if this is reversed the panchama will become the madhyama. Take this fifth relationship down the scale and you have the cycle of fifth. It was the investigation of these two major cycles that led to the development of the twenty-two shrutis of the Indian musical scale. The interval of *sa–pa* which is 3/2 and *sa–ma* which is 4/3, form the dwaya samavada, which is the principal structure of Hindustani music's ragas.

cycle of thirds is the

gandhara route taking the gandhara of shadja and then the gandhara of the gandhara and so on right to the end of the scale.

cymbals are a percussion instrument made from bell-metal or brass. It consists of a pair of round discs which, when struck together, is used in bhajan singing and congregational music.

D

D is the second note of the C-Major scale in Western classical music.

da-dha is the mnemonic of a kind of stroke with the plectrum or the mizrab on the sitar. It uses the index finger of the right hand. *Da* is the sound produced by an inward stroke and *dha* is produced by an outward stroke. The difference in the texture of these sounds is clearly audible.

dad is a Persian word. It means the appreciation of value. It is an expression of appreciation of the spirit of a performance.

dadra is a kind of composition of the light classical kind. The bol *dha-dhi-na dha-ti-na* is a 3-3 time measure. But because of the allusion to the fact that this tala is used for light classical music, talas like RUPAK and KEHRWA are also sometimes referred to as dadra, which has come to mean a kind of song where the measures are equal and the stresses are also equal.

Dagar is the name of a family of musicians who are traditional dhrupad singers and have the leading edge in dhrupad singing today. Their family hails from Jaipur. Dagar bani is one of the four major dialects of dhrupad practised by the Dagar family. The other dialects are Nauhari, Gauhari and Khandalia.

dak is a drum of the dhol type used in North India.

Dakshina Gurjari is a raga mentioned in the *Sangita Ratnakara*. It is supposed to be a subsidiary raga of Raga Gurjari.

Dakshinamurti Shastri was a composer of the post-

Thyagaraja period in Carnatic music. A Telugu Brahmin, he composed several kirtanas in Telugu with the signature Garbhapuri.

damaram constitutes a pair of drums, conical in shape, played with two sticks. One of these sticks is curved and the other is straight. It is largely used as accompaniment to temple processions. It is carried on bullock carts in front of the procession and is played by trained boys.

damaroo is an hour-glass-shaped drum seen in the hands of the dancing Nataraja. A symbol of Shiva, it has parchment leather on its two faces. The knotted ends of two strings tied at the narrow centre of the drum strikes the two ends to produce a rhythmic sound. Damaroo is a drum found in all parts of India.

Damarukapriya is the name of a raga derived

from the thirty-first melakarta, Yagapriya.

Damodar Misra lived in the seventeenth century and wrote the book, *Sangit Darpan*. It was the *Sangit Makarand* and the *Sangit Darpan* that together described the whole concept of raga in Indian classical music.

damper is a mechanical device that stops the string of an instrument from vibrating. It is on account of the damper that it is possible to hear the sound of each note of the piano when struck successively. Each note has to stop vibrating before the next one can be heard.

danda is the crossbar found on the stem of a rudra veena. The two large ground resonators are attached to the danda.

daph is a shallow drum. When jingles are attached to it, it becomes a tambourine. When there are no jingles it is called daph or **chang**.

Darasa Piya is the pen name Ustad Mehboob Khan used in his compositions. He was from the Agra gharana.

Darbar is a janya raga of the twenty-third melakarta, Karaharapriya.

Darbari Kanada is a Hindustani music raga. It is believed to have been discovered by Mian Tansen.

dardila is used to describe a voice or music touched with anguish. The term is derived from 'dard', which means pain.

Darshana Ashtapadi is the nineteenth Ashtapadi in the *Gita Govinda* of Jaideva. A tale is attached to this name. While the Ashtapadi was being composed, Jaideva had stopped composing for a while and gone away. Lord Krishna, it is said, went to his house in his absence in the guise of Jaideva, and taking the manuscript from Jaideva's wife, Padmavati, finished one of the incomplete sections, which later came to be known as Darshana.

Dasari was an expert nagaswaram player of the nineteenth century. Thyagaraja is believed to have praised his music.

dasavatara refers to the ten avataras or incarnations of Vishnu. The Carnatic composers like Jayadeva, Purandara Dasa and Thyagaraja have considered Buddha also as an incarnation of Vishnu. So the ten avataras are Matsya, Kurma, Varaha, Narashimha, Vamana, Parasurama, Rama, Krishna, Buddha and Kalki.

Dasavatara Ashtapadi consists of the first Ashtapadis of Jaideva in which each stanza deals with one of the ten incarnations of Vishnu.

Dasavatara Dhyanam Kirtana is a composition by Thyagaraja that begins

'*Dina Januvana*' in the Raga Bhoopalam of the Carnatic school.

Dasavatara Mangalam is the song '*Mangalam Jayamangalam*' composed by Purandara Dasa. This is in Kalyani raga.

Dasavatara Ragamalika is the well-known kriti '*Kamalajasya*'. The kriti is in ten ragas in the sequence Mohanam, Bilahari, Dhanyasi, Saranga, Madhyamavati, Athana, Nata kurunji, Darbar, Ananda Bhairavi, and Saurashtram. The composition is by Swati Tirunal.

dasavidha gamaka are ten kinds of gamakas described in the *Sangeeta Ratnakara* as part of the panchadasa or fifteen gamakas described in it. These are aroha, avaroha, dhatu, sphurita, kampita, ahata, pratyahata, tripuchha, andola and murchhana.

Dattatraya Palusker was the son of Vishnu Digambar Palusker. He was a popular singer in his time although he died young. His voice was a silvery tenor that had great beauty and appeal. His bhajans were highly applauded and to this day the standard set by the recorded bhajans of Palusker is difficult to equal.

Dattila is the author of the fourth century grantha called *Dattilam*. The *Natya Shastra* refers to him as one of the pupils to whom Bharata taught music. Dattila is a known authority on all matters of music such as shruti, raga and tala. Most musicologists refer to Dattila with veneration and men like Matanga Abhinava Gupta, Raghunatha Gupta and others quote Dattila as an authority. Dattila himself quotes Narada in his *Dattilam*.

Day, C.R. was a captain in the Madras Regiment. He studied Carnatic music while he stayed in Madras and wrote a book called *Music and Musical Instruments of Southern India and the Deccan* published by Novello, London in 1891. It discusses Carnatic music practice, and mentions some of the great musicians of his time. The volume carries colour illustrations. There is also a list of Sanskrit works on music attached to the volume.

dayan is the right half of the tabla.

deem ta deem is the mnemonic of syllables of the tarana compositions of khayals.

Deepchandi is a tala with fourteen matras divided between four unequal sections. In the first and the third sections there are three matras each, while the second and the fourth have four matras each. There are beats on the first, fourth, and eleventh matras. The eighth is empty or khali.

Desh is one of the ragas of Hindustani music. It closely resembles the Carnatic scale of Kedara Gaula. It is a raga of the night and is sung between ten and midnight.

desi means belonging to the country or the desa. The division of music into desi and margi had to be made because of the provincial music developing spontaneously all over the country. It was different from folk music which was popular with the lower sections of society. Desi sangeeta's rules were not laid down or authorised by any external body or external tradition. Its sanction came from the accepted practice of the people who sang them. Margi sangeeta, on the other hand, had strict rules. Desi included vocal and instrumental music and dance as part of one inheritence. There are margi ragas and desi ragas, margi talas and desi talas, and prabandhas both margi and desi.

Devadatta is the name of the conch used by Arjuna in the *Mahabharata*.

dha is the sixth note of the Indian scale and is the abbreviated form of the note, DHAIVATA. It is also the mnemonic for the sound produced when both hands are used to strike the two drums. The right hand hits the kinara or the edge of the tabla, while the left strikes the middle of the bayan. The combined sound of both these strokes is referred to as *dha*.

dhaivata is the sixth note in the scale of swaras.

dhama is the name given to the paste of flour and water that was applied to the left half of the tabla in order to dampen the vibrations. This technique is no longer in vogue.

dhammar is a dhrupad composition composed in dhammar tala. It is also a tala with fourteen matras in four unequal sections. The first beat is the *sam*, the second beat is on the sixth matra, the eighth matra is empty or khali and the eleventh matra is the next beat. Songs sung on the occasion of Holi are in this tala.

dhatu relates to the various movements of a composition. These are sthayi (the first movement), antara (the second), sanchari (the third) and abhog (the final movement). Each of these are conceived as a dhatu of the composition.

Dhenuka is the name of the ninth melakarta raga.

dhin is a mnemonic for both the hands striking the tabla together, the right hand striking the centre of the tabla and the left striking the centre of the dayan. The composite sound is termed *dhin*.

dhir kit is the mnemonic for a four unit set of beats

played together on the two halves of the tabla.

Dhira (Dheera) Shankarabharanam is the name of the twenty-ninth melakarta raga.

dholak (dhol) is a popular drum used to accompany light forms of music like bhajans, ghazals, qawwalis, and a lot of folk music. In the Carnatic school of music, the dholak is used to accompany nagaswaram players and is called dhol. It is an open-air instrument and matches the loudness of tone of the nagaswaram. (See also DAK.)

dhrupad vani indicates the style of dhrupad singing. There are four distinct vanis or gharanas in dhrupad singing. These are Gudiya Govarhar, Khandar, Dagar and Nauhar. Dhrupad is a shortened version of DHRUVAPAD.

dhrut implies a swift tempo. It refers to the fast composition in a khayal and often follows the madhyalaya. The LAYA concepts like vilambit, madhya and dhrut are based on perceptions of tempi for any given piece of music or performance. This is not a mechanically conceived pacing. Dhrut is also referred to as JALAD.

dhruva is a kind of musical composition referred to by Bharata in the *Natya Shastra* and is used in dramas. It also refers to the introductory section of a song corresponding to the pallavi, which is repeated as a refrain at the end of each subsequent section of the song. In the *Gita Govinda* of Jayadeva, this section is often found.

dhruvapad (dhrupad) is a form of Hindustani classical music older than the khayal. It has great dignity and grace of carriage and architecture. It has four sections. It is begun at a slow pace but picks up pace and is later sung in multiples of its basic pace. The four sections are called the asthayi, antara, sanchari and abhog. It is believed that Raja Mansingh of Gwalior (1486-1517) was the father of this type of composition and style of performance. Swami Haridas (1502-), Makarand Mishra, Tansen and others were some of the prominent dhruvapad voices in the past.

dhruva veena is an experimental veena used for demonstrating the twenty-two shrutis in which the pitch of the strings are kept constant. The alternative kind of veena called the **chala veena** is one in which the pitch of the strings is reduced step by step in four stages. The four strings are reduced by intervals of 81/80 256/243 25/24 and so on.

dhuns are those tunes on which many folk and rural songs are based. The emotional content in these tunes provide the basic feel of several ragas. Notionally these dhuns are predominant in Bhairavi, Kafi, Pilu, Khamaj and similar ragas.

dhvani means any sound. In the *Dattilam* it is used to denote the shruti, for the author mentions twenty-two dhvanis in the octave.

diatonic scale pertains to a major or a minor key. This is distinct from the chromatic scale.

diatonic semitone is the purna dvishruti interval with a frequency of 16/15. This is somewhat the same as the interval that separates the antara gandhara and the shuddha madhyama.

dik really means direction. It also stands for the figure ten. Sometimes it is used to indicate the tenth swarasthana which is the dhaivata, the chatushruti in the twelve-note gamut.

dilruba is a North Indian musical instrument with frets played with a bow. It has a near soprano human voice and is often used as an accompaniment. It has nineteen frets which can be moved for minute adjustments. It has four main playing strings and twenty-two sympathetic strings. The instrument is played on the madhyama string and the instrument is tuned to *Sa-Pa-Sa* and *Ma*.

dindi is a Marathi musical form used in kathakalakshepams.

Dipak is one of the six primary ragas mentioned in the *Brihaddarma Purana. Sangita Ratnakara* also makes a mention of this raga. The famous raga with magical powers sung by Tansen is believed to have been in this raga.

dirgha means long—a long note lasting at least two units of time as opposed to a hraswa swara which lasts only one unit beat of time.

disi means ten in the mnemonics of music. It is a bhoota sankhya (musical mnemonics) and is the tenth chakra of the melakarta.

ditone means an interval which has two tones—9/8 × 9/8 and 81/64.

Divyamati is a janya raga of the fortieth melakarta Navanitam.

divyanama kirtana literally stands for the names of the Lord to be sung in his praise. It is intended for congregational singing and consists of one pallavi and many charanas. The tunes often remain the same whether pallavi or charana.

Divya Prabandham is the name given to a group of 400 verses composed by twelve Vaishnava saints. These were in the form of slokas.

doha is a couplet in Hindi sung to music. A doha can also be sung in Bhojpuri or Avadhi.

dohara is a kind of song in Marathi sung in katha kalakshepam.

Doom is a community of semi-professional singers of the Punjab.

do-tara is a two-stringed drone instrument. The strings are tuned to the shadja of the accompanying singer. It has a gourd resonator and stem pegs for tuning.

duff is a small drum which is also called **duffli** and is used in folk music.

dugun is twice the standard tempi of a piece of music. That is, it has two aksharas per beat.

dundhubi is a large drum shaped like a cone, made in olden times from the fibre of a mango tree. It is played with a stick. 'Dundhubi' is a word found commonly in Sanskrit literature denoting a sound of celebration.

Dundhubipriya is a raga, also referred to as Dundhubi.

durbala swaras are those swaras in a raga that are used feebly without stress or obvious repetition.

Durga is a pentatonic raga with the same scale as the Suddha Saveri raga of Carnatic music. In the Hindustani tradition it comes from the Bilawal thaat and in the Carnatic it comes from the Dhira Sankarabharanam melakarta.

dvadasa chakra comprises of the twelve chakras in which the seventy-two melakartas have been arranged. Each of these chakras are made up of six melas. The chakras are Indu, Netra, Agni, Veda, Rutu, Bana, Rishi, Vasu, Brahma, Bisri, Rudra and Aditya.

dvadasa mudra are the twelve kinds of mudras

that figure in musical compositions. The mudras indicate in the text of the lyrics of the composition information like the name of the composer, the name of the raga, the type of composition and the tala it is set to. The twelve mudras are: (i) **vaggeykara mudra** which indicates the signature of the composer; (ii) **swanama mudra** where the composer's name figures in the text such as Thyagaraja, Jayadeva and so on; (iii) **itara nama mudra** where the composer uses a pen name such as Guruguha for Dikshitar, Venkatesa for Pattanam Subramanya Iyer, or Darasa Piya for Ustad Mehboob Khan of the Agra gharana; (iv) **raga mudra** where the name of the raga is mentioned in the text and this is true for all lakshana gitas; (v) **tala mudra** is where the tala of the composition is mentioned in the text, for example, all Raga Tala Malikas as also many Chaturang compositions, which incorporate the bols of talas in the text; (vi) **acharya mudra** is where the name of the preceptor of the composer is included in the lyrics of the composition; (vii) **raja mudra** is when the name of the patron of the composer is part of the lyric; (viii) **prabandha mudra** indicates the type of composition like dhrupad, tarana, kriti and padam; (ix)**nayaka mudra** includes the names of those nayakas to whom the lyric is addressed, for example, 'Mira ke Prabhu' and 'Kahath Kabira'; (x) **sthala mudra** is the name of the shrine or temple in which a deity may be situated—the Tevarams tiruppugazh and Kshetra kritis belong in this genre; (xi) **vamsa mudra** is a mention of the composer's vamsa, kula, gotra or parents in whose honour the composition is made; (xii) **biruda mudra** is the name of the title associated with the composer's lakshana mudra or the name of the substantive lakshana grantha on which his compositions have been structured.

Dvijavanti is the Carnatic raga which closely corresponds to the Hindustani Jaijaivanti. It is derived from the melakarta Hari Kambhoji.

dwaya samavada See CYCLE OF FIVE.

E

E is the third note of the European scale. It is the interval gandhara of the swaras on the Indian scale.

edaka is an hourglass-shaped drum from Coorg in Karnataka. Its body is made of metal and it is used as an accompaniment to Kathakali performances in Kerala.

edda palaka is the name of the wood that covers the top of the bowl of the veena.

Edukula Kambhoji is an earlier name of the raga which is now called Yadukala Kambhoji.

eduppu is a Tamil word which means the point at which the music begins on the tala cycle. The eduppu called sama eduppu begins when the tala and the music begin on the same beat. Atita eduppu is when the music begins before the tala and the anagata eduppu is when the tala begins before the music.

ekadandi veena is a veena in which the sounding bowl and the stem of the veena are made from a single piece of wood. The head piece alone is made from a separate piece of wood joined to the rest of the veena.

eka dhatu divyanama kirtana is a kirtana where the pallavi and the charanas have the same dhatu or tune. The famous Yadukula Kambhoji of Thyagaraja that begins '*Sri Rama Jayarama*' is an example.

ekantavadyam is an instrument like the veena whose sound is so mesmeric that it can be heard and enjoyed in solitude.

ekaraga mela veena is a

veena which can play a raga belonging to one mela at a time. This veena has moveable frets and when the mela changes, the frets have to be moved to handle the next raga. In contrast to this veena there is the sarvaragamela veena in which the frets are fixed and naturally there are more frets. The grantha named *Sarvamela Kalanidhi* of Ramamatya makes a mention of this veena.

ekashruti dhaivata is the note *dha* interval of the Indian scale. It corresponds to *A* of the European scale of the frequency 128/81. This is the dhaivata used, for instance, in Raga Saveri. It lies just one step above the interval panchama and just below the shuddha dhaivata or the komal dhaivata of the system of twenty-two shrutis.

ekashruti rishabha is the interval *re* or the note

D of the European scale. Its frequency is 256/243 and is used in Raga Gaula. This is the interval just above the shadja and immediately below the shudha rishabha or what is komal rishabha of the scale of twenty-two shrutis.

ekatantri is a one-string veena whose sounding bowl is made of coconut shells.

ektal is a twelve-matra tala cycle. The first, the fifth, the ninth and the eleventh have beats on them. The third and the seventh matras are the empty or khali beats.

ektara is a one-string tanpura whose sounding bowl is made of gourd and is attached to a bamboo stem. It gives a tonic drone and is associated with mendicants seeking alms and carries overtones of sacrifice and homelessness—the spirit of the bairagi.

Elanka Manohari is a janya raga of the thirty-seventh melakarta named Salagam.

Eman Kalyan (Yeman Kalyan) is a raga in the Hindustani tradition. It is sung at dusk. It is a raga of the sixty-fifth melakarta, Mechhakalyani. It is a sampoorna-sampoorna raga and all its notes are tivra.

equal temperament is a system of tuning adopted for keyboard instruments like the piano. In this the octave is divided into twelve equal semitones. The Indian scale is based on what is called the just intonation based on the natural untempered scale.

esraj is a stringed instrument that is mostly played in Bengal. It has frets but is played with a bow. Like the sarangi, the bowl is placed on the floor and the stem on the shoulder. The instrument also has sympathetic strings and it sounds almost like a human voice and is much admired as an accompanying instrument.

Ettiyapuram has been an important place for music in South India since the second decade of this century. Musicians like Muthuswamy Dikshitar, Baluswamy Dikshitar and Subbarama Dikshitar have been named as asthana samasthavidwans from this town. The maharajas of this town have been great lovers of music and some have been noted composers. The *Sangeeta Sampradaya Pradarshini* was published by the Ettiyapuram Samasthanam in 1904. Ettiyapuram is also the birth place of Subrahmanya Bharati.

ettugada pallavi is another name for the charana of a varnam. When the swara sangatis in the final stages of a varnam are concluded with the charanam, that charanam is called ettugada charanam.

F

F is the name of the fourth note of the European scale. It is the interval *ma* of the Indian scale.

F holes are the sound holes of the violin and the cello. The holes look like the letter 'F' in shape.

Fai(y)yaz Khan (1886-1950) was one of the greatest names in the Hindustani music tradition. He was of the Agra gharana. His voice was a rich and piercing baritone. He was honoured with the title Aftab-e-Mousqi meaning the 'sun of music'. His style was a magical mixture of dhrupad and khayal in both of which his music displayed haunting power. He sang thumris with great appeal. For years he was the premier musician attached to the court of the Maharaja of Baroda and in many of his compositions he used the *nom de plume*, Darasa Piya Prema Piya. He trained many musicians among whom the well-known names were Dileep Chandra Bedi, Pandit S.N. Ratanjanker and Asad Ali who, after the partition of India, lived in Pakistan. (See AGRA GHARANA)

fankar means a creative person or an artist. It is the Urdu equivalent of the Hindi word 'kalakar' and is the standard term for an artist.

faran jatisara are the characteristic patterns of rhythmic figures played at a swift pace on drums. The great dholak player Nannu Mian of Pudukottai Samarasthanam was a well-known player of these faran jatis on his dholak.

farodast is a tala with thirteen matras and is distinctive for not having an empty beat or khali position in the cycle. Its beats are on the first, the third, the fifth, the seventh and the tenth matras of the cycle.

Farrakkabad baj is a style of tabla playing which, with the Ajrada, Benares and Lucknow styles, forms what is called the Poorab baaj. The name derives from two towns, those of Farrakkabad-Ajrada, twin townships that were famous for their abilities for making laya variations on the tabla. The Ajrada is better known as a style for dance accompaniment.

fiddle is the colloquial name for the violin.

fife is a small shrill-toned flute. It is blown from the side and is part of the fife and drum duo in Western music.

fifth note is the panchama interval of the Indian scale.

figure is a musical pattern. It is noticed in recurring symmetries in swara passages such as the chitta swaras.

finger-board is the stem of the violin over which the strings pass and which are pressed by the fingers to produce musical notes. The finger-board may be plain as in the violin or the sarod or fretted as in the veena or the sitar.

finger holes are the holes of a wind instrument which are stopped either with fingers or by keys.

fingering is the technique of the use of fingers in any musical instrument.

firat is associated with firat ki taan. The first is usually at least at twice the tempi of the standard madhyalaya tempi and its passage uses coupled notes, two at a single beat.

flageolet is a small wooden wind instrument whose one end has a mouthpiece.

flageolet tones are the natural harmonics of stringed instruments. These sounds have a flute-like quality hence the name flageolet.

flute is considered a nearly divine musical instrument on account of its associations with Lord Krishna. Between the veena, mridangam and the venu, it is the venu or the flute that enjoys a pre-eminent position in the hierarchy of musical instruments. It is among the oldest instruments known in India and consists of a hollow bamboo cylinder with finger holes and a blow hole. The Indian flute is a simple cylindrical tube of bamboo, one end closed, about fourteen or fifteen inches long, unlike the European flute which is made usually from grenadilla wood or the Cocus. The European flute has keys whereas the Indian flute has no keys. There are flutes made of ivory, ebony, sandalwood, iron, bell metal, silver and even gold. The flute is classified by the way it is held. The transverse side horizontally held, is also the side blown through, ara the direct flute which has a mouthpiece is also called the beak flute on the basis of its mouthpiece. The vertical flute is the pan type. Famous flute players include Pannalal Ghosh and Hari Prasad Chaurasia in the Hindustani tradition and Ramani, Mahalingam and Palladam in the Carnatic school.

folk music is the music of the masses of the nation. The Indian folk musical tradition is very close to its classical inheritence. Besides being bewilderingly rich and varied in a country with a single culture, spread across marvellously varied lifestyles and geographical and ethnic traditions, the folk song and dance tradition form a bottomless mine of rich and creative vitality. There is a folk song associated with practically every event in life. Rites of passage, festivals, seasons, each has a distinctive form of music associated with it. The classical idiom, at least in the north of India, has a strong and obvious connection with folk music in the travel of ragas from place to place, in the origin of gharanas, in the dialects used by different gharanas. That the language of music is Brij and Bhojpuri, Dingal and Malwi and the Khadi boli of Hindi proves classical music's connection with the folk tradi-tions of India. Among the subjects of folk songs are pilgrimages and marriage; there are songs on medicine or therapy; there are funeral songs, songs that tell the stories from the Puranas; there are comic songs on deities, satires of village and country, songs on weaving and basket-making, songs propitiating snakes, labour songs, lullabies, songs for games, songs containing proverbs, songs of love and courting.

fundamental note is the plucked sound of the whole string.

G

G is the fifth note of the European scale, which is the pancham of the Indian scale.

ga is the name of the third swara in the Indian scale. It is called gandhara, whose solfa name is *ga*. The Hindustani scale has only two gandharas—the natural or shuddha gandhara and the komal which is the flat gandhara. According to the Carnatic classification there is also the komal sadharana gandhara which is 32/27, the sadharana gandhara 6/5, the antara gandhara 5/4, and the tivra antara gandhara which is 81/64.

gabguki is a stringed instrument used in the south as accompaniment.

gadya means prose as opposed to PADYA which is verse. In a musical composition, a libretto may be prose, gadya, or verse, padya, or a mixture of both gadya-padya.

Gagana Bhoopalam is a janya raga of the twenty-first mela which is Kirvani.

gamaka is the generic nomenclature for all graces and ornaments. It is ideal when the gamaka is unconsciously incorporated as an expression of feeling or meaning. In the Hindustani tradition, there are several varieties of gamakas— meend, andolan, ghaseet and muddit. There is an essential difference between the Carnatic and the Hindustani tradition in the use of gamakas. In the Carnatic tradition the gamaka is an essential part of the melodic structure. It is rare therefore that in this tradition you hear a swara unadorned and plain. In the Hindustani tradition, the gamakas are personal and communicate a personal message in the raga, so that there are musicians who use the graces sparingly depending upon the emphasis or subtlety they wish to produce. It is possible to make an understatement and use innuendo in Hindustani music. In Carnatic music the use of gamaka is extolled. Stillness is rarely used to communicate meaning and feeling. Since the gamakas are the chief identifying features of the ragas in Carnatic music, they cannot be omitted or reduced at will. In Hindustani music even the tonal characteristic can identify the raga without any gamaka whatever. In this sense Hindustani music is plainer and less ornamented compared to Carnatic music. Gamakas exist everywhere in the Indian musical tradition—in Vedic chants like Narada Siksha and in both religious and non-religious music. The ten excellences described in the ancient texts include Sukumara, Rakta, Poorna, Alankrita, Sama, Madhura, Vyakta and Prasanna. Matanga uses the word gamaka in music for the first time and as the ragas had come into existence in his time, the gamaka is basic to a raga. Various commentators have described several numbers of gamakas. Haripala in his *Sangeeta Sudhakara* describes seven gamakas. Narada in his *Sangita Makaranda* describes nineteen gamakas, Sarangadeva describes fifteen gamakas, Govinda Dikshitar Venkatmukhi and several others have dealt with the gamakas mentioning varieties of approaches to this subtle treatment of swaras. The fifteen well-known ones are as follows: tiripu, sphurita, kampita, lina, andolita, vati, tribhinna, kuruja, ahata, ullasita, plavita, gumpita or humpita, mudrita, namita, misrita. These apply to both instrumental and vocal music in both traditions.

Gambhira Nattai is a janya raga of the thirty-sixth mela also called Gambhira Nattai.

gana is a single foot in prosody.

Gana Bhaskaram is a Telugu work by Srinivas Iyengar published in 1934.

gana krama is the style of singing various movements in a composition. The gita is sung right through without repeating any line. In the kriti on the other hand, each sangati is sung twice. The anupallavi is sung after the pallavi and the charanam follows the anupallavi.

gandharva is a singer from heaven and appears in numerous places in the Puranas and mythologies of Indian religious life. They attract by the strange other-worldly power of their voices. The term 'gandharva' has been used in Hindustani music in naming some of its singers. Kumar Gandharva was named Gandharva for the strangeness of his musical prowess by a wandering sadhu passing through his native home. Sawai Gandharva and Bal Gandharva are other examples.

Gandharva, Bal was one of the most gifted singers of the Marathi stage and was responsible for the vitality, power and appeal of Marathi natya sangeet. His role was always of the female lead and his voice, an alto tenor, was supple, trained and coleratura in style. His music was classically derived and some of his songs from dramas like *Saubhadra* and *Manapaman* have been part of the cultural folklore of Maharashtra.

Gandharva Veda is the branch of the Veda that deals with music. It is an Upa Veda or a subsidiary Veda along with Ayurveda, Dhanur Veda and Artha Shastra.

Garbhapuri See DAK-SHINAMURTI SHASTRI.

Garudadhwani is a janya raga derived from the twenty-ninth mela, Dhira Shankarabharanam.

Garudapriya is a janya raga derived from the forty-fifth mela, Subha Pantuvarali.

gat is the musical figure on which instrumental music is built. Mnemonics are often used in building a gat. For example *dara dir darada* are mnemonics that have power and sub-tlety. Sitar and sarod and the tala instruments all have bols on which these gats are built.

gati indicates the tempi of a piece, the speed and the gait of a composition. Vilambit, madhya, dhrut or jalad are all gati descrip-tions.

gatra veena is another term for the human voice. It is the veena (implying music, sound) of the gatra, which means the body.

Gautama was one of the early authorities on music mentioned in old works on music.

gavantu is the term for the ledge of ivory that separates the body of the veena from its stem.

gavaiyya means a singer. It is a colloquial expres-sion.

gayaka is a singer.

gayaki means a singing style. An imitation of a vocal style produced on an instrument is often called a gayaki ang. The in-strumental approach to music is transcended and the instrument is made to sing as though with a human voice.

gayatram is a song or hymn, structured in the metre of the gayatri, which is a popular fourteen syll-able mantra.

gayatrin is one who sings hymns.

geet is any piece of poetry that can be sung as a song, as distinguished from a BANDISH.

Geetila is a collection of songs.

gejjai is the sheaf of ankle bells tied round the feet of bhagavatars and dancers and even actors who sing and explain and dance. Professional dancers consider the gejjai in high regard as being the symbol of their life. When the gejjai is presented to a dancer, it is an event of great importance and indicates the ability to dance professionally. It is a symbol of graduation in the art.

getti melam is a colloquial term meaning vigorous, loud music often played by a group of musicians in a band, in a nagaswaram troupe or even a brass band. This kind of music is played at the moment the mangalsutra is tied round the neck of a bride when getting married.

gettuvadyam is a subsidiary tala instrument played during concerts. It has three strings and is tuned to *sa-pa-sa* and is played with sticks. It is played on open strings.

geya natakam is a kind of opera. It is a costume drama with the music woven in and made one with the action.

ghada is also known as a matka. It is an earthenware pot used to play the rhythm. It is integral to the folk music of the Punjab. The ghatam of Carnatic music is the same thing and accompanies as a subsidiary percussion in a concert.

ghadiyal is a brass plate that is hung on a frame. When struck with a wooden stick it booms.

ghana ragas are ragas whose principal characteristics are easily revealed. Ragas such as

Arabhi, Nattai, Varali, Sri and Gaula are ghana ragas.

ghana raga malika varna is a varna in which the ghana ragas come and go in a raga malika fashion. The varna of the famous veena player Kuppayyar is of this construction.

ghana raga pancharatnam is a popular Thyagaraja composition of the five ghana ragas. These are in Adi tala and each of the kritis is several charanas long. The charanas are sung as swara sahitya. The five pieces are *'Jagadananda Karana'* in Nattai, *'Dudukugala'* in Gaula, *'Sadhinchene'* in Arabhi, *'Kankana Ruchira'* in Varali and the famous *'Endaro Mahanubhavolu'* in Sriraga.

Ghana Tarangini is a janya raga of the twenty-ninth melakarta, Dhira Shankarabharanam.

ghana vadya are percussion instruments made of metals like gold, particularly cymbals.

ghar means home. It is also the name of a point on the edge of the right hand piece of the tabla. The tabla is fine-tuned from this position.

gharana is a school or style of singing in Hindustani music. The ragas of Hindustani music have distinctive characteristics that change with gharana, and these may derive from the place of origin of a style, distinctive voices, the style of singing and the approach to music. These styles are known as gharanas. These have names from various towns and cities of India where the guru who first espoused the style lived. So you have names like Agra, Jaipur, Gwalior, Bhendi Bazar, Rampur, Kirana, Indore, Sham Chaurasi, Vishnupur and so on.

ghaseet really means pull across. But unlike the

MEEND which is also pulled through, the impact sought here is not that of reaching the other note but that of the journey. It is a smooth transition from one note to another without actually touching the interim notes. It is the portamento in Western music as distinct from the glissando, in which the interim notes are touched in passing.

ghatam is a large round earthen pitcher used to keep the laya in Carnatic music.

ghazal is a form of Urdu poetry that is often sung. The first couplet of this form is called matla and the finishing couplet is called makta. The remaining couplets are called misra and antara. Each couplet of a ghazal is complete in itself and does not need the other couplets to complete its meaning or to expand it.

ghudaj is the bridge on the sitar over which the strings pass. It is often made of ivory or bone.

ghunguroo is a clutch of bells fitted on a flat belt which is tied to the ankles of a dancer. These are often made from base metals and often silver or even gold. There could be anything from 50 to 250 bells per ankle in a ghunguroo.

gidda is a folk dance of the Punjab danced together by three or four girls, keeping rhythm clapping their hands.

Giridhara is a janya raga of the twenty-eighth mela, Harikambhoji.

Giriraja Kavi was the grandfather of the great composer Thyagaraja. He was born in Tiruvarur and was a gifted composer. He was a musician of the Tanjore court and composed many yakshaganas, and many compositions on Vedantic themes.

gita (gitam) is a musical composition, among those

first taught to students who have completed their training in swara exercises and alankaras. These are simple melodies in ragas in uniform laya and usually sing the praise of God. Many well-known Sanskrit shlokas are sung in the form of gita. Before Thyagaraja came on the scene, musicians were fond of singing gitas. There are two kinds of gitas—the sanchari gitas and the lakshana gitas. The lakshana gitas also describe the characteristics of the ragas in which they are composed. Gitas do not normally have angas like pallavi, anupallavi or charanam. They may, however, have sections.

Gita Govinda is an immortal classic composed by Jayadev in the twelvth century. There are twelve sargas in it, composed in Sanskrit. Each song contains eight verses or padas or charanas on account of which the group is called the ASHTAPADI. There are twenty-four songs. The Ashtapadis were composed before Indian music divided into its two styles—the Hindustani and the Carnatic—and was sung across the subcontinent. The nayaka-nayaki bhava in the worship of God was its main characteristic. The Ashtapadi songs are what are known as dvidhatu praband and consists of two sections or movements—the udgraha and the dhruva, which later became the PALLAVI and the CHARANAM.

gitanugam is any instrument used as an accompaniment to a singer, for example, violin, sarangi, esraj, veena and so on.

gitkari is in the same family as KHATKA or MURKI and is a grace and ornamentation in a raga.

go is the syllable for the third mela of a chakra in the sankhya mnemonics of the seventy-two melakarta scheme.

gobbi is a kind of folk dance with girls and boys dancing in a circle, clapping and waving their hands. The songs that are sung for these dances are called gobbi pattu.

godha is a bow string described in the Rig Veda.

godhika is a drum in which alligator skin is used. An alligator in Hindi is called a godha.

Golconda is a place near the city of Hyderabad in whose fortress the composer Bhadrachala Ramdas was imprisoned.

Golconda Padusa was the patron of KSHETRAYYA, the famous composer of padas. Kshetrayya composed 1500 padas in Golconda in the space of forty days and was honoured by the ruler.

gomukha is a wind instrument used for military purposes, mentioned in the *Ramayana* and the *Mahabharata*, shaped like the mouth of a cow. Hence the name.

Gopal Naik was a leading musician in the court of Allauddin Khilji (1295-1315). A great composer and singer, he wrote several treatises, important among them being *Tatarnavam Raga Kadambakam* and *Graha Swara Prabandham*. He was a contemporary of Amir Khusro who admired him. On one occasion he hid behind Allauddin Khilji's throne and copied out the various phrases and styles of alap used by Gopal Naik and later reproduced a perfect copy of the singer. The king and Gopal Naik and the courtiers were stunned at this exhibition. The two remained close friends.

gopichand also called nandin, is an instrument made of bamboo with only one string, and is mainly an ektara.

gotu is the shortened name of GOTTUVADYAM.

gottuvadyam is a stringed instrument like the veena. It is also known as mahanataka vina. It was supposed to have been best for dramatic performances because of the loud volume of its sound. The name is of Tamil origin. The instrument has no frets and therefore has a liquid tone and needs a perfect ear to play. Since there are no frets there is no lateral deflection of the strings as in the veena which has frets. The strings of the gottuvadyam have a higher tension than the veena. There are eight strings and three tala and drone strings. The five playing strings are the sarani strings, the remaining strings are the panchama, mandra and anu mandra. There are also sympathetic strings beneath the playing strings. A stick is used to slide over the strings to produce the various notes. The playing strings are plucked downwards and the tala strings are plucked upwards.

Govindacharya wrote the grantha *Sangraha Chudamani* in Sanskrit, perhaps the last on the Sanskrit granthas of lakshana. The author lived in the latter part of the eighteenth century. He lived in the Tanjore court. The *Sangraha Chudamani* is available in a modern published version.

Govinda Marar (1798-1843) was from Travancore and was a gifted singer. His reputation stemmed from his accurate shruti focus and awareness of the need for purity of notes. Another characteristic was the speed of his vocal techniques. His fast passes were swift and sonorous at the same time. He invented a seven-stringed tanpura which had two pancham swaras, two sarani swaras, two anu saranis and one mandra position of the shadja. There is the well-known episode of Marar singing *'Chandana Charchita'* at the Tiruvaiyar Thyagaraja festival in the Raga Pantuvarali. This composition was sung in ati vilambita, which converted an eight matra tala into forty-eight matras. The accuracy of his tala made a great impact. He is reported to have doubled, tripled and hextapuled the speed retaining the sharp clarity of the song. Thyagaraja himself is said to have been deeply impressed.

graha bheda is the technique of finding new raga scales by shifting the tonic note of a raga. This is achieved by shifting the shadja of any scale. For example, if you take the raga Malkauns whose scale is *Sa Ga Ma Dh Ni Sa* and make the *Ga* into a *Sa*, the resulting scale becomes the scale of Durga which is *Sa Ri Ma Pa Dha Sa*. It is a simple mathematical relationship between the notes of a scale and is one of the essential substances of the Western musical tradition. Musicians like Bade Gulam Ali Khan used swarabheda sparingly but indicated their prowess in the method by their ability to sing these scales through the most fluid transitions. But while this can be done by well-trained musicians who have a sound awareness of this method, musicians like Gulam Ali Khan considered techniques such as swarabheda in Raga Vidya as vainglorious exhibitions of ability and irrelevant to the raga. So while in short phrases in the concluding sections of a performance they displayed these techniques, they used such technical exercises in proportion and never allowed these values to enter their view of ragas, which were never treated frivolously as mere scales.

graha trayam is a term that indicates that there are three broad grahas in musical compositions. The sama graha is one in which the music begins with the sama position of the tala avarta. The anagata graha is where the piece begins after the sama, after a lapse of 1/4, 1/2, 3/4 aksharas of the tala. Atita graha is the composition that begins after the sama of the avarta.

grama literally means a town. There are three gramas—shadja grama, madhyama grama and gandhara grama. This was the earlier approach to scales before ragas were assimilated into music. The grama murchhanas used to be prevalent at that time. The madhyama grama meant fixing the shadja on the madhyama. The gandhara grama and the madhyama grama paved the way for ragas with tivra or prati madhyama ragas where the F-sharp enters the scale.

granthee is a person who reads the Guru Granth Saheb in the gurudwara, the Sikh temple.

Gudiya Govarhar (See DHRUPAD.)

Gujjari is a janya raga derived from the fifteenth melakarta, Mayamalavagaula.

gul is Persian for flower. This is a word that makes reference to the musical features of the qawwali.

guru is one of the six angas of Carnatic music. It has two matras or eight akshara kalas. This word also means guru as preceptor, who takes the student from darkness to light. 'Gu' means darkness and 'ru' means to shine forth.

Guru Basava was a great composer of devotional songs in Kannada. The Kannada tradition has been contributed by singers like Sripada Raya (circa 1500), Purandara

Dasa (1484–1564) and Kanaka Dasa (circa 1550).

Guruguha is the signature of Muthuswami Dikshitar.

Gurumurti Shastri Paidala (circa eighteenth century) is among the greatest composers of gitas after Purandara Dasa. He was a great singer and enjoyed wide fame.

Guru Poornima also known as Vyas Pooja, is the day for the worship of the guru. Poornima means the full moon day. Guru Poornima falls on the full moon day of the month of Ashadh.

Guru Purandara Vithala is the signature of the younger son of Purandara Dasa (1484-1564) used in his compositions.

gurumukh vidya implies learning from the lips of the guru. This refers to the oral tradition from which the traditional system of transmission has arisen.

guru shishya parampara indicates a line of preceptors. It is the tradition that transmits the art through a preceptor.

Guttila is a famous musician who appears in the Jataka tales of Buddhism. Lord Buddha is believed to have been Guttila in one of his earlier births.

Gwalior has been the seat of music for centuries. Raja Man Singh of Gwalior (1486–1517) started this tradition of music in his kingdom. He is believed to have been the founder of the dhrupad style of singing. The great musician Mian Tansen's tomb is in Gwalior. The Tansen festival is celebrated in Gwalior and is remembered the way Salzberg remembers Mozart.

Gwalior gharana is one of the oldest gharanas of Hindustani classical music.

This gharana has affected the music of all other gharanas and is often referred to as the mother gharana. Among its stylistic features is the use of a middle tempo speed even in the vilambit laya of bada khayals and an organization that has finely worked bol taans and bol baants. Many other gharanas are believed to have been born out of the devices of the Gwalior gharana, for example the Rampur Patiala and so on. The Vishnu Digambar gharana is of course the very essence of this gharana. Nathan Peerbaksh is supposed to have been the progenitor of this gharana. Other well-known names include Bade Mohamed Khan's two sons, Haddu and Hassu Khan, Bade Nissar Husein Khan, Balkrishna Buwa Ichalkranjiker (1849–1926), Vishnu Digambar, Krishna Rao Shankar Pandit, Rajabhaiya Poochvale, Shankar Rao (1863-1917).

H

Haha is the name given to a celestial musician who figures in ancient literature.

hahakar is a term coined by Ustad Amir Khan to describe a kind of broad and raucous intonation that is loud and coarse.

Haimavati is a janya raga of the nineteenth melakarta, Natabhairavi. It sounds like Durga or Suddha Saveri when instruments play it.

Halebid is a place which is famous for musical iconography. Its statues show musical instruments of ancient times. These and other sculptures make the Halebid and Belur temples among the most exquisite in South India.

Hamir in the Carnatic tradition is the same as Hamir Kalyani. In the Hindustani tradition Hamir is of the Kalyan thaat and in the Carnatic it is a janya of the sixty-fifth melakarta, Mechakalyani.

Hamsadhwani is from the twenty-ninth melakarta, Dhira Shankarabharanam. It is a highly popular raga of the Carnatic school and is becoming increasingly popular in Hindustani music. Its principal attraction is that its scale gives plenty of opportunities to modulate. For this reason it is described as a murchhanakaraka raga.

Hamsanandi resembles Raga Sohoni of Hindustani music. It belongs to the fifty-third melakarta, Gamanashrama.

Hamsanarayani has two origins. One from the Marwa thaat and the other from the Poorvi thaat in the Hindustani tradition.

The Carnatic Hamsanarayani resembles the Poorvi thaat raga of the Hindustani tradition. It is a janya of the fifty-first melakarta, Kamavardhini.

Harballabh was a musical faqir of the nineteenth century. A music festival is held in his memory at the saint's samadhi at a place called Devi Talao in Jallandhar in Punjab.

Haridas is the name of a saint who asked Thyagaraja Swami when he was about eighteen years of age to recite 'Rama Nama' 860 million times. It is said that Thyagaraja was able to complete this number in twenty-one years. In the Telugu opera *Nauka Charitram*, Thyagaraja pays homage to this saint who transformed his life. This discipline made every song he sang or verse he composed seem self-evident and final.

Haridasa Swami is the well-known musician saint of the Gosain parampara. Born in the city of Multan in 1537, Swami Haridas made Brindawan his home. He was a great bhakta of Lord Krishna. Tansen of Akbar's court (1556–1605) was among his most well-known students. Swami Haridas died in 1632 and his Jayanti is celebrated every year at Brindawan with music performances both in the Hindustani and Carnatic styles.

Harikambhoji is like the Hindustani Khamaj in scale. There is no raga by that name in Hindustani music. In the Carnatic system Harikambhoji is the twenty-eighth melakarta, often also called the Haridaragaula.

harmonics refers to tones. A stretched string when plucked produces a sound which is called the natural harmonic and if it is stopped at any point on its length and then plucked, the sound produced is called an artificial harmonic. The full string vibration is also called the fundamental note of the string or the first harmonic. The stopped strings produce upper partials and harmonics. Harmonics are called SWAYAMBHU-SWARAS, that is notes born of themselves.

harmonium is a portable organ-like instrument that has bellows which are pumped using the hands or feet. Its scale is tempered. This instrument is believed to have been brought to India by missionaries.

harmony is the overall pleasant awareness of sounds played together in consonant notes.

haveli sangeet refers to bhakti songs. Jayadeva of the Ashtapadis or the Ashtasakhas of dhrupad are examples of this style of singing. Havelis are the old houses where such music used to be sung. This kind of music belongs in the Vishnusampradaya.

Haya lila is another name for the *Turaga Prabandha*, the grantha which contains the names of the 108 talas.

hechhu sarani is the name of the highest pitched string of the tala strings of the veena.

Hemakriya is a janya raga derived from the twentieth mela, Natabhairavi.

Hemant is a raga composed by Ustad Allauddin Khan of Maihar. It belongs to the Bilawal thaat.

Hemanta is the name of a Hindustani musician who went to South India and challenged Banabhadra, the court musician of Madurai, during the reign of Varaguna Pandyan. Lord Shiva, the story goes, appeared as a woodcutter servant of Banabhadra and sitting under the room of Hemanta, sang the Raga

Sadari and impressed Hemanta so much that he left the city the next day, not daring to sing and challenge Banabhadra when even his servant sang so well.

hem-khem refers to the knowledge of a musician. Two ragas Hem Kalyan and Khem Kalyan are closely allied ragas whose distinction is so difficult to see only a master can produce that indisputable characteristic which separates the two ragas. Hem is a compound of the ragas Kamod and Suddha Kalyan and Khem is a compound of Kamod amd Yeman Kalyan.

heptatonic scale is a sampoorna scale like Bhairav or Mayamalavagaula.

hexatonic scale is any six-tone or shadava scale like Malkauns or Mohanam.

Hindustani sangeet is the system of music prevalent in the north of India. The southern part of India is supposed to have the Carnatic system. Both have as their foundation the concept of raga in which they are one. Another common point is the fact that both the north and the south uses the swara, which is a vocal utterance, as the basis of its ragas, whereas the West uses the notes which are mechanically conceived and are connected with the frequency of tuning forks and an equally tempered scale.

hoonkar is a vocal humming exercise which enables the singer to get a fine vibrant timbre. It is practised with the mouth closed.

Hori is a form of light music of the thumri category. The lyrics of Hori almost always relate to the festival Holi which is a festival of colours celebrating spring. The festival has deep connections with the rasa lila of Radha-Krishna. These are sung during the season of Holi in the months of February and March. Hori Dhammar is a Hori sung in the tala dhammar and Hori Kafi just another form of the word Hori. The terms hori and dhammar are often used interchangeably. Ragas like Kafi, Jhinjhoti and Khamaj form the raga system of Hori and require from the singer a well-trained and feeling voice. Dhrupad singers usually also sing dhammar compositions and the subtle variations of double, triple and quadruple measures of dhammar are part of this style of singing.

hrswa means short. It is the opposite of DIRGHA which is long in duration. Hrswa is usually the length of one unit of time, and dirgha would be two units of time.

Huseni in Hindustani music is believed to have come from Muslim sources and has certain groups of swaras from the Hindustani raga Deshi or Desi Todi but is hardly ever sung. In Carnatic music it is a raga which is highly popular and is a janya of the twenty-second mela-karta, Karaharapriya, which is the Hindustani Kafi thaat.

I

ida is the name of a particular configuration of taans of the sa grama made up of five notes—*Ni, Dha, Ma, Ga, Re.*

idai surungu is an hourglass-shaped drum with parchment on its two faces. A thin tape along the narrow part can be squeezed to strain the strings that tie the parchment on its two faces. This raises the pitch or lowers it, giving the sound a characteristic intonation. It is played in temples.

idakka is a drum from the Malabar coast of Kerala. This has an hourglass-shaped resonator made of wood. Strings fasten the two parchment discs mounted on its two sides. By gripping the strings the player is able to alter the frequency of the sound and a whole octave can be played on the instrument with sticks.

Indisa is a raga sung in Kathakali music.

Indore gharana is supposed to have started with Chhange Khan whose grandson was the famous Ustad Amir Khan. They came from Kalanaur in Haryana and settled in Indore. The Bhendi Bazar and the Kirana gharanas were the inspirations for this gharana. It is based on the merukhand system. Ustad Amir Khan was among its notable sons in this century and admired Ustad Abdul Wahid Khan and Ustad Rajjab Ali Khan of Devas for their mastery of the Merukhand. On account of these circumstances the Indore gharana has a very rich and variegated awareness of raga. The musicians of this gharana who continue to flourish are Pandit Amarnath,

Srikant Bakhre, the Singh Bandhu, Gokulotsav Maharaj and Poorabi Mukherjee.

Indu is the name of the first chakra of the seventy-two melakarta scheme. It comprises of the first six melas.

interval is the ratio of the frequency of a note to the next lower note in Western music.

Iraqi mode is one of the modes used in Iraq and has the same scale as the twenty-second mela, Karaharapriya.

Iryuman Tampi (1783–1858) was a musician and composer of the court of Travancore. He is reputed to have been the author of several Kathakali plays such as *Dakshayagam, Kichaka Vadham* and *Uttara Swayamvaram*. He has composed several varieties of varnams such as tana varnams, pada varnams and several kirtanas.

israj is the name of a bowed instrument like a sarangi but with fixed frets, like the sitar. In Urdu it is called DILRUBA, and taos in Persian. Its sound is close to the human voice and is an excellent accompaniment for singers of classical music.

itara mudra is the signature that a composer uses in his compositions, which is not his name. Muthuswami Dikshitar identified his composition by the signature, guruguha. Pattanam Subramanya Iyer used Venkatesa. In Hindustani music you have the case of Bade Gulam Ali Khan who used the word Sabrang to identify his compositions. Mohamad Shah called himself Rangile which has become a distinguishing signature of the Agra gharana. Sadarang was Niyamat Khan and he popularised the khayal style of singing. (See MUDRA.)

J

jaan is used in the sense of a kind of weight and life in a singer or player of an instrument.

jabra means the jaw which some singers use in their vocal enunciation. It is often accentuated in taan sequences. Many schools disapprove of this use of the jaw in singing.

jabra ki taan is the kind of singing that uses the jaw to articulate the fast passage of notes. It is a widespread technique of singing at a fast pace across the scale and has a curiously attractive characteristic about its motion. There are several singers who use this technique of musical expression.

Jagadekamalla is the twelfth century composer of the grantha *Sangita CC Chudamani* in Sanskrit. He was from the Chalukya dynasty.

jagah means place in music. In Tamil it denotes the place in the tala cycle where the composition begins. It is also called graha or EDUPPU.

Jaganmohini is a janya raga derived from the fifteenth mela, Mayamalavagaula.

Jaipur gharana is also known as the Atrauli or Kolhapur gharana. Ustad Alladiya Khan was its major figure. Other names are Munji Khan who died in 1937, Burji Khan who died in 1950, Bhaskar Rao Bhakle, Kesar Bai Kerkar, Moghubai Kurdiker, the mother of Kishori Amonker, Govind Rao Tembe (1881–1955), Dilip Chandra Bedi, Malikarjun Mansur, Nivritti Bua Sarnaik and Kishori Amonker.

jalad means quick. It is a

tempo that is double the measure of the madhyalaya or four times the measure of the vilambit laya. (See also DHRUT.)

jalectromonium is an instrument invented by Pappu Subha Rao. It is a harmonium whose keys are connected electrically to the cup of a jaltarang, and when the harmonium is played the keys also hit the cups so that two sounds are simultaneously produced—of the harmonium and that of the jaltarang. A switch can disconnect the harmonium from the jaltarang.

jaltarang literally means water waves. The taranga is composed of china cups of various sizes filled to various levels with water and tuned to the twelve notes of the scale. When struck with sticks after tuning, the cups give a pleasant ring and are often used in small ensembles with the violin and the mridangam. The tuning of

the instrument takes a long time and involves adjusting the water levels in each cup. The dexterity to play this instrument is considered to be among the chatushashti kalas or the 64 arts.

jamjama is an Urdu word that is used to describe the use of two notes repeatedly in any length of elaboration.

janaka-janya is the classification of ragas into parent and derivative ragas. It is based on a genus-species system. The janaka ragas have all the seven notes up and down the scale while the janya need not have all the notes. Some are omitted in various combinations up and down the scale, or one way up the scale and another way down the scale.

janaka raga literally means a parent raga. The three conditions for a janaka raga are that it should be SAMPOORNA both up and down the scale. It should not have any VAKRA in it. The same notes that ascend must also descend. There are 72 janaka ragas. (See also MELAKARTA.)

Janasammodini is a janya raga derived from the twenty-eighth melakarta, Harikambhoji.

janta swaras are double notes like *Sa-Sa, Re-Re, Ga-Ga* and s on. These are part of the scale exercises of classical music.

janya raga is a raga derived from a parent scale. (See JANAKA-JANYA above.)

jati is the name adopted on the Katapayadi classification of twelve chakras. Jati Ata tala has an avarta with eighteen aksharakalas. Jati is also the name given to the mnemonics of tala such as *taka tari kita naka* and so on. It also means the emotional colouring of a swara.

Examples are Dipta, Karuna, Madhya, Neera and so on. Jati has its connotation in raga. Bharata Muni mentions them as the ten LAKSHANAS or attributes of a raga such as graha, tara, mandra, nyasa, apanyasa, alpatwa, bahutwa, audava, shadava, sampoorna. (See also BOL and BRIHADDESI.)

jatiswaram is a composition that has no words but has divisions such as the pallavi, anupallavi and charanam. Sung in sargam or solfege, it is used widely in dance and has several movements.

java is a V-shaped piece of hard string inserted on the forefinger of a sarod player to strike the string of his instrument.

javali is an erotic song that is earthy and sensuous. The word originates in Kannada and signifies a kind of lewd poetry. It is distinguished from the PADAS in which love is treated with gravity. In javali love is light, provocative and flippant. The popularity of the javali lies in the bright and attractive tunes in which it is sung. Javalis are composed in well-known ragas and are of mid or slow tempo.

jawari is the point where a thread is inserted between the string and the bridge of a tanpura where the string resonates best. This is a technique applied to give texture to the sound of the string of the tanpura over and above its accurate focus. It also denotes the bridge over which the strings pass before it is stretched across the length of the instrument and then tied to tuning pegs at the other end. This is an Urdu word and its Sanskrit equivalent is MERU.

Jayadeva is the well-known romantic poet and composer of the *Geeta Govinda*, which continues to thrill singers and listeners to this day. He

was born in the state of Orissa in a place called Kendulo about forty-eight miles from the city of Puri, in the Kakarpur thana. A Brahmin by birth, he lived in the court of King Lakshma (1116 AD) of Navadwipa, which is modern Nadia in Bengal. The *Geeta Govinda* has been translated by Sir Edwin Arnold into English and is entitled 'The Indian Song of Songs', sometimes also referred to as the Sanskrit Song of Solomon.

Jayammal was the daughter of the famous Veena Dhanammal. She was a finely trained singer with a large repertoire of kritis, padas and javalis and was well-known for her clarity and bhava. Balasaraswati, a great dancer, was Jayammal's daughter.

Jayjaywanti is a raga in the Hindustani tradition and has affinities with the Carnatic Raga Dwijavanti.

jazbaat is the introduction of emotion in music.

Jew's harp is a rhythmic instrument, also called the MORSING.

jhala is the fast paced section of an instrumental compostion played on a sitar or sarod or any of the usual stringed instruments. It is a rhythmic use of the CHIKARI strings of the instruments that produces the sound of ankle bells, adding to the resonance of the main melody. Several laya patterns are played on this.

jhampa ghapu is an ancient tala measure of five aksharakalas for each avarta.

jhanj is a pair of brass cymbals used in temple service. About eight inches in diameter, it produces a dramatic clang.

Jhanjhamritam Subbayyar was a nineteenth century musician who could sing in three octaves with ease. He was given

the title Jhanjhamritam by the Mysore Samasthanam.

jhaptal is a ten metre cycle tala. It has unequal sections divided into two or three or two and three units of matras. The first matra is the sam, the third is the first beat after the sam, the sixth is the empty khali beat and the eighth is the third beat of the cycle.

jhumra is a tala that has fourteen matras divided into two and three matra sections and two and four matra sections. The first beat is the sam, the fourth has the next beat, the eighth is the empty beat or the khali and the eleventh is the third beat.

Jinjhoti is a raga that belongs to the Khamaj thaat in Hindustani music which is the Harikambhoji melakarta. It is also called Chinchiruti in Carnatic music.

jiva is also known as the JAWARI. It is the fine thread that goes beneath

jiva

85

the bridge and strings of a tanpura. Its texture and quality are enriched by this means and gives the tanpura that enveloping sound which is vital to the music of the raga.

jiva prabandhas are those compositions that are timeless whether because of their musical quality or their poetry. Jayadeva's *Ashtapadis* belong in this genre.

jiva swara is the note in a raga which gives the raga its principal power and attraction. This could be a NYASA swara of the raga though not necessarily. In Raga Saranga the shuddha madhyama, which is a foreign swara, is also the jiva swara.

jod is that stage of an alap when the laya is brought into the alap in a manner which gives the alap a special lift and a language. When from the vilambit tempo an instrumentalist moves his alap to the mad-hyalaya or medium tempo, this transition into the new tempo is called jod. This kind of alap is performed principally on instruments and in the *nom tom* alap of dhammar and dhrupad. This is what is called the jod-alap which, while emphasising the laya, is slightly slower in pace than the usual jod of instruments.

joda is the name given to the two middle strings of the tanpura, both of which are tuned to the shadja of the octave.

Jogiya is a Hindustani raga belonging to the Bhairav thaat, the Mayamalavagaula mela. The Carnatic Saveri is similar to Jogiya.

jugal bandi is a performance of two instrument players or singers. It spaces out a performance, dividing its progressions in a shared manner. In the Carnatic tradition, this is termed jodi pattu.

K

Kabir was one of the great Bhakti poets of the North. Born in 1398, he was a believer in the equality of all religions and the single spiritual substance of man. His bhajans are widely sung both popularly and by classical singers. Kumar Gandharva was among the most notable names of Hindustani music who sang the nirgun (without attributes) and the sagun (with attributes) varieties of bhajans and gave a distinction to that form of singing.

kacheri is the Tamil word for a concert or any musical entertainment.

kacheri dharma includes the duties and obligations, rights and privileges of musicians performing in a concert, its organisers and the audience. This entails everything from dress, mode of address and welcome to the seating arrangements on the platform.

kadan is the sound produced by the combined strokes on the two halves of the tabla.

Kadana Kuthuhalam discovered by Pattanam Subramania Iyer (1845-1902) is a janya raga of the twenty-ninth mela Dhira Sankarabharanam. The most famous composition in this raga is '*Raghuvamsa Sudhanbudhi*'. It has an orchestral quality and is lively and is scale-like in its nature. There is a lovely chittaswara section in the composition which is believed to have been put into it by the composer's contemporary, Tiruvaiyar Subramania Iyer.

kafea is a part of the qawwali. It is a verse that rhymes.

Kafi is the name of the

thaat in Hindustani music corresponding to the twenty-second melakarta, Karaharapriya, of Carnatic music. The Raga Kafi is born from this thaat and uses both the shuddha gandhara and the shuddha nishada.

kahaka is an ancient musical instrument.

kahla is a wind instrument made of a precious metal like silver or gold or even copper. It has an oboe like sound.

kajari really means black. Also called the kajali, it is a folk style of music of Uttar Pradesh sung during the rains. It is a light classical form of music and uses the tales of Krishna and Radha for inspiration.

kakali nishada is the shuddha nishada of Carnatic music. This is slightly higher than the shuddha nishada of Hindustani music, as the swara is fixed by feeling. This in turn makes the tivra madhyam of Carnatic music slightly higher than its counterpart in Hindustani music.

kakapadam belongs among the six angas that are usually part of musical time measures. It consists of a ghata, which is a single matra or beat, a patakam, a krsya and a sarpini. Its symbol is a '+' sign. The kakapadam figures in the tala named Simhanandana, which is the tala with the longest cycle. (See ANGA.)

kaku is a swara technique that emphasises the significant characteristic of a raga. Parswadeva's *Sangeeta Samaya Sara* describes the kakus, which are six in number: (i) raga kaku is the essential splendour of a raga; (ii) swara kaku is the embellishment of a raga through the quality and shading of its mukhya swara through gamakas or mere vocal power; (iii) desa kaku is the ability to bring regional inflections into the raga giving it a richness which is strange and novel; (iv) anya raga kaku is the contrasting quality achieved by the slight traces or hints of other ragas within the raga being sung. This effect can be readily achieved by graha bheda techniques or bhavas of other ragas; (v) kshetra kaku emphasises all the rules of the raga in various permutations and combinations; (vi)vadya kaku is a technique of bringing an instrumental quality into the expression of ragas.

kala means art. It can also mean the basic unit of time.

kaladharma denotes the code of observances associated with music and performance.

Kalahasti is the signature of the composer Veena Venkataswami Raja of Kalahast. '*Tana Varna Valachiyunna*' in Push-

palatika Raga is a composition of Venkataswami Raja and has this signature.

kalakantha means one with a sweet voice.

kalakshepam means spending time. Kathakalakshepam is derived from this and is a musical discourse of the stories from the *Ramayana* and *Mahabharata*. The kalakshepam combines music with storytelling and scholarship.

Kalanidhi is the name of the grantha on *Sangeeta Ratnakara* by Kallinatha.

Kallinatha is the author of the commentary on Sarangadeva's *Sangeeta Ratnakara*. Kallinatha lived in the fifteenth century. KALANIDHI is the name of this commentary.

kalpita melakarta is the name given to Venkatmukhi's nineteen melas out of the seventy-two he had already postulated. These nineteen were already popular when the classification was carried out. The remaining fifty-three were academic in nature at the time as these had not been used in compositions until then.

kalpita sangita is composed music. Kritis come under kalpita sangita.

Kamavardhini is the fifty-first melakarta. It is the old name for Pantuvarali. This raga is first mentioned in the *Sangita Chudamani* of Govindacharya.

kampita (See PANCHADASA.)

kana is a small additive note that is not quite a KHATKA.

Kanakangi-Ratnangi (See BAHATTARA MELAKARTA.)

kanjira is a tambourine used in Carnatic concerts.

kankani is the outer rim, usually of horn, that joins the stem of the veena or tanpura or the gottuvadyam to its bowl.

Kansen is a playful variant on the word Tansen, the great musician of Akbar's court. This term is used to indicate those who become great lovers of music but cannot sing themselves. Here the word 'kan' is used to indicate the ears. The ability to hear and enjoy music is the main identification of people who cannot sing but greatly appreciate the art.

Kanthe Maharaj was among the greatest tabla players of the Benares gharana. His sons, the famous Kishen Maharaj, and the late Godai Maharaj also known as Samta Prasad, gained great fame.

kapat taan is a taan that deceives the ears.

Karaharapriya is the twenty-second mela raga. It corresponds to the Kafi thaat of Hindustani music. The great musician of the

Kirana gharana Ustad Abdul Karim Khan has recorded the song *'Rama nee sama mivarum'* in this raga. This is the primordial scale of Indian music.

karakhat is a harsh tonal quality in the voice.

kartal is a pair of wooden cymbals played by holding them in the hands. It is used to accompany bhajans.

Kashalkar Vishnu Annajee (1884–1968) was among the senior students of Pandit Vishnu Digambar Paluskar. He was among the earliest musical evangelists sent out by his guru to settle in Allahabad and propagate Hindustani classical music. He was among the most widely honoured musical gurus of his time and made Allahabad a key city among the musical capitals of the first half of this century.

katapayadi sankhya is a system of mnemonics that is used to determine the serial numbers of words. This used to be widely used in astrology, music, and several other arts and sciences in India. This is a mathematical or a numerological approach to the letters of the Sanskrit alaphabet. Each letter of the Sanskrit alphabet has a serial number. These are summed up in three key phrases. Kadinava is a series of nine letters beginning from 'Ka' and ending in 'Jha'. The next is Tadinava which is a series beginning with 'Pa' for five letters ending with 'Ma', and Yadyashta is a series of eight letters beginning with 'Ya' and ending with 'Ha'. The letter 'Na' is zero. The names of the seventy-two melakartas are based on a formula derived from the katapayadi sankhya. The formula can be illustrated with an example. Take the Mela Ramapriya. Rama indicates the katapayadi syllables. The serial number of 'Ra' is two, and that of 'Ma' is five, making for 25. This number has to be reversed, which gives the figure 52, which is the serial number of the Melakarta Ramapriya.

kathak is a dance form of North India. It originated in the temples and has nritta, nritya and abhinaya in its expression. These dancers are experts in music, dance and storytelling, hence the name 'kathak', derived from 'katha'. The *Mahabharata* refers to kathakas. There are two major centres of kathak—Lucknow and Jaipur. The music to which this dance is performed is light classical.

kathakalakshepam is another form of kalakshepam or passing time. Katha added to the term implies spending time telling stories. These are the stories of the Puranas told through songs sung in dramatic fashion with power and resource. The *Ramayana*, the *Mahabharata*, and *Bhagavatam* form the basis of the stories and anecdotes that are sung and recited by the kalakshepam performers. Tanjore Krishna Bhagavatar is described as the father of kathakalakshepam (1847–1903). These recitals need scholars to perform, not just musicians.

Kathakali is the dance form of Kerala. Also known as Attakatha, it is based on the *Natya Shastra*. Kathakali is extremely masculine in its technique. The story is fully acted out, scene by scene, through mudras. The make-up of Kathakali is elaborate and the colours used have symbolic significance. More than two hundred plays have been written for Kathakali. The authors of Kathakali compositions include Raja Kottarakara, Unnayi Warrior, Swati Tirunal, Iryuman Tampi and others.

keertan is a style of devotional singing in which the main refrain is sung by the congregation in unison, with accompanying instruments like manjeera, ektara, harmonium, and kartaal. It was in the sixteenth century that keertan singing became popular with the saint Chaitanya Mahaprabhu (1485–1533) in Bengal. The leader of a keertan session is called a keertankar.

kehrwa is a tala of four beats, the bol for which is *dhagi na dhinaki dhina.*

keli kottu is the prelude to a Kathakali performance, announcing the show later in the night.

Kerala Kalamandalam is the academy established by poet Vallathol Narayana Menon to give systematic Kathakali training to young aspirants. The Academy is situated at a place called Cheruthuruti near Trichur.

Kesarbai Kerkar was among the most well-known and well-loved musicians among women singers in this century. She belonged in the Jaipur gharana and was a disciple of Ustad Alladiya Khan. Endowed with a powerful voice her art had presence and lasting appeal. Her style was witty and forceful with a deceptive simplicity. Rabindranath Tagore gave her the title, 'Surashree'.

khali means empty and stands for the empty beat in a tala cycle, also called a nissabda kriya. A tala or a beat measure is cyclic and always returns to a designated point of emphasis called the sam. The cycle has a squeezing and a relaxing quality, squeezing to the sam and relaxing to the khali.

khalifa means the chief. In the guru-shishya parampara, the musical heir of the guru is often referred to as a khalifa.

khamsa means 'holding

five'. The word's roots are in Persian. It refers to any religious poem that has five verses or sections to it, and is usually applicable in a QAWWALI.

khan is the grace that barely touches either of the neighbouring notes on any position on the scale. For example, a khan on the shadja will use *Ri* or *Ni* on either side of the shadja and touch it so subtly that the note merely flexes at that point.

khand means a section and in music refers to those sections of a tala cycle into which it is customarily divided. In teen taal its sixteen beats are divided into four equal sections or khands. The first is the most heavily accented beat, the second is less accented and the third is open or khali and the next is equal in emphasis to the second beat, finally returning to the most accented beat, the sam, which brings it back to the first beat of the tala cycle

Khandar vani is one among the four vanis in dhrupad singing. Khandar vani belongs to the Bikaner area of Rajasthan. (See DHRUPAD.)

Khan Saheb is the way a king in Afghanistan is referred to. This form of address is used to indicate respect when Muslim musicians are addressed.

kharaj is the name given to the bass section of the scale. It is the lowest note that a voice can reach for whichever register. It was a name given to the shadja position of the scale and was usually one octave lower that the standard singing level of the average tenor voice. Vocal exercises for training timbre, steadiness and other qualities are developed through a series of exercises in this region of the scale. (See ANUMANDRA.)

khatka is a grace which in a two-note span, gives

edge, sharpness and speed to the figure. It forms part of the triad—khatka, murki, and gitkari. Based on the swara *Sa,* for example, a khatka will be *Sa Ni Ri Sa.*

khayal is a word of Persian origin meaning 'imagination'. It is believed to have developed out of the qawwal style of singing and through the period of Amir Khusro became an important part of the Hindustani music tradition. The arrival of the khayal, which slowly displaced the old dhrupad style of singing, effected a revolutionary change in the Hindustani classical music tradition. The khayal's structure requires a high order of improvisational skill in the musician at several levels and layers of the raga. The range and scope of improvisation covers the whole range of human experience from the mystic to the frontiers of mathematical and intellectual exploration. It is among the most challenging musical forms in the raga inheritence of the subcontinent. The tradition uses all forms of musical expression such as alap and sargam, bol and boltan, gamakas and khatkas, asthayee and antara. The curious paradox in the tradition of the khayal is the circumstance that the level of the art is rarely the level of musical accomplishment of the musician but a measure of the human essence. This makes the art piquant in a novel way. Khayal also implies dhyana which means meditation.

khayal gayaki is the overall format of the khayal, its parts which have certain definitions, its sections, the way it grows, and so on. It does not mean the characteristics of gharana which too are part of the khayal.

khol is a mridangam-shaped drum made of clay,

narrowing down its right side. It is used to accompany bhajan singing.

kinar means the edge and refers to the edge of the tabla which produces the sound whose mnemonic is *na* or *ta*.

Kinnara is the name given to a community of celestial musicians who play instruments. These are the instruments of the gods and are believed to accompany the Gandharvas who are celestial singers. Kinnara is male and Kinnaree is female.

kinnaree is a stringed instrument like the veena. The Biblical Kinnore is a similar reference.

Kirana gharana derives its name from the place Kirana near Saharanpur in Uttar Pradesh. The style of Kirana is distinctive with a vocal quality of gentle repose. Its raga elaboration has a distinctive design as it builds up. This style is called BAR-HAT. Abul Wahid Khan, Abdul Karim Khan and Sawai Gandharva are some of the famous names of this gharana. Today Pandit Bhimsen Joshi is the chief exponent of this style.

kitt is a mnemonic of the tabla played with both hands on the tabla. *Ki* is played with the full palm flat on the left half of the tabla and the *tt* follows with three fingers of the right hand on the right half of the tabla.

kolattam literally means play with sticks. It is among the most popular forms of folk dance in the south. It is danced in a group with the natural choreography that emanates from the rhythm and the music. The temples of Rameshwaram, Tirupati and many others have friezes that show groups of girls dancing a kolattam.

komal implies the flatter pitch. Literally, it means

soft. It is the opposite of TIVRA which means the higher or the sharper pitch.

kombu means horn or shringa. It is a brass instrument, four to six feet in length, crescent-shaped, with five brass tubes of varying diameters. When blown, it gives a loud and shrill note and is used in temple processions. The sound of the kombu is believed to have a welcoming quality.

koot taan means a complicated and extensive set of notes in complex figures in a taan.

Kovur Pancharatna consists of five kritis composed by the great composer Thyagaraja in praise of the deity, Sundareswara, in his shrine at Kovur near Madras. These are 'Sambho mahadeva' in Raga Pantuvarali, 'I vasudha nivarti' in Sahana raga, 'Kori serunipa rare' in Karaharapriya, 'Nammuni vachlina' in Kalyani and 'Sundera varuni' in Shankarabharanam.

krama means regular. The phrase krama sampoorna means a straight arohana and avarohana without tortuous variations. Shadava krama would mean a six-note regular and audava krama would describe the regularity of the five-note scale.

Krishna is associated in music with the venu or the divine flute. He is also called by several other names such as Muralidhara Venugopala, an incarnation of the Lord Vishnu in Dwapara yuga of the Hindu cosmic epoch. The pure music as ascribed to Lord Krishna is believed to be the essence of Indian music. Composers and musicians have used this figure of Krishna with his flute from the dawn of Indian memory. Krishna appears as an inspiration in Jayadeva's Ashtapadi in the *Geeta Govinda*, the songs of Meera, the songs in Brij, and in thumris and khayals. The entrancement of Krishna's music pervades the art and is difficult to separate from its inspiration.

Krishna Lila Tarangini is the longest Sanskrit opera. Narayana Tirtha composed this opera. This contains 112 cantos while Jayadeva's *Geeta Govinda* contains 12 sargas. Its origin is in the Bhagavatam's *Dasamaskandam* which begins with the avatara of Krishna and ends with Krishna's marriage to Rukmini. It is counted among the LAKSHYA GRANTHAS on raga and rasa.

kriti is one of the most highly evolved forms of musical composition in the Carnatic school. Every composer in the Carnatic school has attempted to compose kritis and contributed richly to this form of music. Literally, 'kri' means fulfilment, meaning 'him that does'. Kritis form the bulk of musical compositions in Carnatic music today. Unlike the KHAYAL in Hindustani music, the kriti is a fully composed piece of music, complete in its architecture and motion. Its value lies in its musical content while its sahitya is relatively unimportant. Although the great Thyagaraja and the other members of the trinity have given this form of music so much vitality and vigour, the sahitya has gathered a certain sacredness which musicians accept and observe. The kirtana lays a lot of stress on the sahitya. The kriti has three movements the PALLAVI, the ANUPALLAVI and the CHARANAM. There could be more than one charanam. The kritis are ornamented with several technical devices such as chitta swaras, madhyamakala sahitya, swarakshara sangatis, solkattu swaras, swara sahitya and so on.

kriya is a mode of counting time. There are several kinds of kriyas. The NISSABDA kriya which is silent and the MARGA kriya and SASABDA kriya. These too have nissabda sections.

kshana is the smallest division of time that can be conceived in a kala or between two beats.

Kshetrayya / Kshetragnya lived in the seventeenth century. He was a contemporary of Venkatmukhi, the well-known musicologist. The padam form was invented by Kshetragnya. The quality of his literary gifts and the structural integrity of his padams makes his position in Carnatic musical lore the same as that of Thyagaraja and Purandara Dasa. Both raga and rasa find exquisite description in his padas. A Telugu Brahmin, he was born in the village of Muvva in the Chittoor district in Andhra Pradesh. His compositions have the signature 'Muvvagopala'.

Kudu Kudimiyamalai is a musical inscription on a rock face in Pudukottai, Madras. It belongs to the seventh century, and was inscribed by Mahendra Varman, a Pallava king. Not taking into account incomplete inscriptions in Titumayam and Pudukottai, this inscription at Kudimiyamalai should be considered the only one of its kind in all of India. This inscription belongs to the period before Hindustani and Carnatic music took slightly different paths and therefore can be said to belong to both the traditions. It gives brief SANCHARAS of seven ragas—the Madhyama Grama, the Shadava, the Sadharita, the Panchama, the Kaisikamadhyama and the Kaisikinishada. The sancharas are given in four note steps of taans, in what is known as the Chatushprahara Swaragama.

Kumi is a folk dance performed by girls clapping their hands to keep rhythm. It is performed during marriages and could even accompany the singing of bhajans. There is always an even number of members participating, and their number is generally more than eight.

kural is a Tamil word that denotes the voice or the shadja of ancient Tamil music.

Kusa and Lava were the sons of Rama and known as great singers and balladeers of note who sang the *Ramayana* and enthralled the court of their father King Ramachandra of Ayodhya.

L

La is the Western nomenclature for the sixth note of the Western musical scale which, in terms of interval, would be the swara dhaivata in Indian music.

Laccha Saakh is a raga supposed to have been discovered by Amir Khusro. It belongs to the Bilawal thaat which is Dhira Shankarabharanam. Considered to be a mixture of Bilawal and Jhinjhoti, its lineaments touch on several ragas like Khamaj, Kedar and Gaud Sarang and is often understood to be a raga that has characteristics of these five ragas.

ladant literally means a fight. It is the combative quality used in music to interpret two phrases either individually by the singer, or between accompanying instruments in a concert, or a singer and his tabla accompaniment.

laggi is the term used to denote mnemonics of talas played at a high speed. Talas like Dadra or Kaharwa, when played in accompaniment to lyrics of a thumri or some other form of light music, give an opportunity to double and quadruple the tempi in a few cycles of teentala and its allotropic forms. This gives the lyrics a heightened rhythmic and lyrical appeal and brings to a climax the earlier tempi. Mnemonics like *dhatir, kitathika, dhatin, tatir, kitathika* and *tatin* are examples of the mnemonics of laggi.

laghu means one of the shadangas or six angas that reckons musical time. It consists of a beat and a variable count of fingers. (See ANGA.)

laghu gayaka vrinda means a small choir. The

brihat gayaka vrinda would be a larger choir.

laghu gottuvadyam is a small GOTTUVADYAM with a short stem and only five strings.

laghu veena is a shorter veena, accomodating only about one and a half octaves. It has five strings.

Lajwanti is a raga in the Bilawal thaat. It is a rare raga. In the Carnatic tradition it resembles Suddha Saveri, which has the same scale as Durga.

lakshana is a science or grammar and refers to the raga, the bandish and its characteristics. The lakshanas include aroha-avaroha, jiva swaras, nyasa swaras, raga ragali prayogas, visesha sancharas, subtle shrutis in it, rasa and time of singing.

lakshana geet indicates the main characteristics of the raga in which a song is composed, its arohana-avarohana, the time of day in which it should be sung and so on.

lakshanakara is another term for a musicologist. He is deemed to know a lot of facts about music and is an authority on it. But rarely is a lakshanakara also a capable musician.

lakshana prabandha is a composition in which some laws of music are described in its sahitya. The Murcchana Karaka Mela Ragamalika is a case in point.

lakshya gnyana is the knowledge supposed to exist in a person who learns music by listening. Such people are accurate in their understanding of music and are capable of singing like a vidwan although they have never trained under a musician.

lakshya grantha is a treatise on the science of music. It also has notations of some compositions.

langar in Hindustani

means an anchor and refers to the stabilisation of a performance. In Carnatic music it refers to the ring that holds the thick metallic string that passes over the horizontal rod that is attached to the top of a veena or a gottuvadyam.

langhana is a note that is lightly touched in a raga. The gandhara in Raga Arabhi is a case in point. The shuddha madhyam in Yeman Kalyani is often used as a langhana. It is an example of ALPATWA.

Lanka Dahan Sarang is a Hindustani raga of the Kafi thaat. The Karaharapriya mela, Kanakavarali, bears a resemblance to this raga in Carnatic music. Other ragas like Shuddha Velavali and Shree Raga also bear a resemblance to this raga.

lasya stands in opposition to TANDAVA. It means a female delicacy and is related to dance. Tandava is male and virile. It is the delicacy of a musical phrase.

lava is a unit of time in tala and has a duration of eight kshanas. This is also the name of one of the two sons of Rama. He and his brother Kusa sang the *Ramayana* in the court of their father.

lavani is a Marathi folk song sung to the accompaniment of several instruments like harmonium, drums and pipes. There are many Tamil songs composed in the lavani style. Some of these songs have a conventional format with subtle philosophic themes.

Lavani Chala is the name of a raga figuring in some Purandaradasa compositions.

laya literally means to merge. The term also refers to tempo and indicates the speed and gait of a piece of music in the form of a regularly repeated beat at a recognizable speed. The vilambit laya is slow, the madhya laya is medium paced and the dhrut laya is fast. There is also a term maran laya which is so slow that it is likened to death.

layakar is a person who is a master of laya but not necessarily of tala.

layakari is the play of multiples of the basic laya or tempo. This could be in double or triple or quadruple measures and also those odd multiples of three and five. It is also an opportunity to show examples of the Western tempo rubato which steals and restores the matras of a cycle in various fascinating proportions.

laya mittu refers to the technique of plucking the tala strings of the veena. This is an upward stroke of the little finger on the tala strings, the three strings of which are tuned to the tonic, the fifth and the tonic again.

laya vadya is a musical instrument capable of providing the beat in concerts. The tabla, the ghatam, the mridangam, the kanjira and the tavil are all examples of laya or tala vadya.

ledger lines are those extra lines used in staff notation which are outside the compass of the staff. This is used in music for Indian films, which is often raga-based.

leit motiv is the German term whose English equivalent would be leading motif and relates to a theme played to denote a particular character in an opera. It is often played repeatedly and is used frequently in Wagner's operas. In Indian opera too the entry of a character is often typified by a particular raga or tune or even an instrument. For instance, Krishna's entrance is signified with the playing of the flute, and Narada's with the veena.

linguaphone is an instrument fitted with tongues that vibrate in different swaras when plucked. The morsing is an example. It has a 'metal tongue that is held in the mouth and is made to vibrate the laya of a concert. Often bamboo wood, bone and metal are used as tongues.

lithophones are musical instruments made of stone. There are several varieties of such instruments, including stone pillars that sound all the seven notes of the scale when struck, and certain mukhavinas, which are miniature nagaswarams.

Lochana Kavi lived in Mithila towards the end of the fourteenth century. He is the author of the grantha *Raga Tarangini* and quotes Vidyapati, the poet of Mithila, at the time of the Emperor Shiva Singh. Lochana Kavi recognized the 22 shrutis and enumerated twelve thaats.

His shuddha scale was Kafi (or Karaharapriya of Carnatic music).

logical nomenclature is a structure of naming that has a logical and closely reasoned basis. The 72 melakartas of Carnatic music are an example of logical nomenclature. The names of the 12 chakras are based on the bhuta sankhya and each name shows its precise serial number. Thus 'indu' which means moon, of which there is only one, is the first chakra. The second is called 'netra' which means eyes of which there are two and so on.

lohaja is the sound emanating from metal. It denotes, for instance, the sound produced by cymbals.

loka dharma (See under NATYA DHARMA.)

lute is a stringed instrument which has frets with a resonator that is shaped like a pear. The strings are plucked with the fingers. The Vedic veena is a lute.

lydian is a scale of ancient Greece which corresponds to the Shankara-bharana scale of Carnatic music and the Shuddha Bilawal of the Hindustani scale.

M

ma is the fourth note of the Indian scale. It is the *fa* of the solfa of the European scale. It is also referred to in full as madhyama.

madagam are the pegs or screw pins of the ancient instrument yazh by turning which the tuning of the strings could be adjusted.

madanti is the name of the first shruti of dhaivata in the time-honoured nomenclature for the twenty-two shrutis.

maddalam is a barrel-shaped concert drum. These are of two kinds: the suddha maddalam has a standard elongated shape and the kavana maddalam is more rounded.

Madhavi is the celebrated dancer figuring in the Tamil epic *Silappadikaram* (second century AD) and the mistress of Kovalan, the hero of the poem.

Madhukauns is a raga in Hindustani music belonging to the Kafi thaat.

Madhumadhavi is a raga mentioned in the *Sangita Makaranda* of Nárada which can be sung at noon. It is an audava raga. Madhumadhavi seems to have been the earlier name for MADHYAMAVATI.

Madhumad Sarang also called Madhyamadi Sarang is a raga belonging to the Hindustani music tradition. It resembles the Madhyamavati raga of South Indian music.

Madhumalati also called Madhuvanti, is a raga in the Hindustani music tradition.

madhura is the name of the first shruti of rishabha in the nomenclature for the 22 shrutis as listed by

Bhavabhatta in his book called *Anupa Sangita Vilasa*. It is also one of the ten excellences of gana mentioned in the *Narada Siksha*. This indicates sweetness in singing.

madhura bhakti is that form of devotion where all human beings (male and female) regard themselves as nayakis and worship God as nayaka. Madhura bhava is spiritualised love. This is a sweeter and easier method of approach to God. Thousands of songs have been composed on the theme of madhura bhakti in Sanskrit, Telugu and Tamil. It stands in opposition to VAIRAGYA BHAKTI or stern and austere devotion.

Madhura Dhwani is the other name for the Hindustani raga DURGA.

Madhuri is a Hindustani raga that belongs to the Khamaj thaat. There is no Carnatic raga by the same name.

madhya kala sahitya indicates sections in Carnatic compositions like kritis that are composed at twice the basic tempo. The madhyama kala usually appears at the end of the anupallavi or the charanam or sometimes between each. Such sections give the whole kriti a trim finish. Many Muthuswami Dikshitar compositions include such sections.

madhya laya means medium tempo. (See LAYA.)

madhyama grama is one of the old scales of which there were three. The other two were the shadja grama and the gandhara grama. The madhyama grama is as follows: Sa(1) Ri (10/9) Ga (32/27) Ma (4/3) Pa (40/27) Dha (5/3) Ni (16/9). (See GRAMA.)

Madhyamavati is a janya of the twenty-second melakarta, Kharaharapriya. It bears a close resemblance to the Hindustani MADHUMAD SARANG.

Madras is the southern Indian city considered the Vienna of Carnatic music. Quite apart from the leading role played by Madras as a centre where Carnatic music standards are set and sometimes adjudicated, the city has seen some of the greatest musicians and scholars in action. Several hundred names can be mentioned among those who shed lustre to this city through music including Veena Dhanammal, Tiger Varadachari, M. S. Subbulakshmi and many more. It is a city that has evolved an annual festival of music and the many sabhas introduce new singers and musicians and felicitate well-known ones. The Madras Music Academy has grown into a musician's Vatican where musical values are often articulated. In the Hindustani tradition, music is more diffused, although several cities are now associated with major music festivals. A city of music like Madras is, however, difficult to locate in the case of Hindustani music.

magudi is a musical instrument used by snake charmers. It is called punji in North India. This instrument is polyphonous. A bottle gourd attached to a double cane pipe is cut in reeds. While one of the pipes gives the basic tonic which it produces in a constant drone, the other pipe is able to play the tune. This pipe has finger holes that can be stopped just as in a flute. The wind that enters is blown out through the other end of the bottle gourd. Its sound is melancholy and is normally tuned to the scale of the South Indian Punnagavarali, a kind of Mishra Bilaskhani Todi of Hindustani music. This scale is said to attract serpents. The southern magudi is unable to produce the top shadja of the upper octave. But the North Indian punji, being longer, is able to produce the upper shadja.

Mahalingam T.R. was one of the most brilliant flute players of the Carnatic style. He gave his flute recital such a distinct personal quality that his kind of flute playing is called the Mali style. His tonal purity and his rhythmic ingenuity gave his music countrywide popularity. He was a prodigy by all standards, having begun to play the instrument with enormous classical repertoire by the age of ten.

Mahameru Swami belonged in the nineteenth century and was appointed samasthana vidwan of the State of Travancore. His vocal range was believed to be in the range of three and a half octaves.

Mahatandava is one of the most celebrated dances of Nataraja. A statue of this Mahatandava exists in the temple at Tenkashi in the district of Tirunelveli. This is a giant statue and has sixteen arms, one of which holds a bell, another a single stringed veena and yet another holds a damaru with its two strings with their strikers on its two faces.

Maha Vaidyanatha Iyer (1844–93) is considered to be a Mozart of the Carnatic tradition in music. He was born in Vaiyucheri near Tanjore. He studied under a disciple of the great Thyagaraja, M. Venkatasubbaiah. His father was Panchanada Iyer. Thyagaraja is said to have heard him sing and blessed him. Vaidyanatha Iyer possessed a strangely compelling voice with incredible harmonics and had one unbroken register right across from the anumandra pancham to the ati tara shadja. He sang mostly by MANOD-HARMA.

maheeya means a lover as used in songs from the Punjab region.

Maihar gharana originated in the town of Maihar in Madhya Pradesh. The town went down in history through Ustad Allauddin Khan who settled in Maihar, one of the greatest sarodiyas of his time. The Khan sahib's famous shishya, Pandit Ravi Shankar, son Ustad Ali Akbar Khan and daughter Annapurna Devi made the Maihar gharana an enormous presence in Hindustani music. Ustad Allauddin Khan started the Maihar band which became well known all over North India.

major scale is the principal scale in which Western music is composed. In the Indian classical tradition it connotes the Shankarabharanam scale of Carnatic music and the Bilawal scale of Hindustani music.

Makarand Pandey is often considered to be TANSEN'S Hindu name. But there is also a theory that this was Tansen's father's name.

makta is the concluding couplet of a ghazal.

makuta swara means a crowning swara pattern. It generally denotes the string of sargam, which are solfa syllables at the end of each section of a Ragamalika, connecting it with the next raga.

Malgunji is a Hindustani raga of the Kafi thaat. Its rough Carnatic equivalent is the Raga Natakurunji which, however, has only the shuddha gandhara.

Mali is the popular name by which the flute maestro T.R. Mahalingam was known. (See MAHALINGAM.)

Manarang was the pseudonym used by Bhupat Khan, a well-known composer of the Gwalior gharana. He was the son of Sadarang and lived during the reign of Mohamed Shah (1719–1748).

Mand is a raga of the Bilawal thaat or Dhira Shankarabharanam melakarta. Many Rajasthani folk songs are in this raga. The popular Marathi bhajan *'Thakur tava sarana'* and the Carnatic *'Janaki manoharam bhaje'* are in raga Mand.

manda gati is a slow movement. This is demonstrated in all vilambit laya compositions.

mandal is a drum used widely among tribal people.

mandaram is the name of the lowest pitch string of the tanpura tuned to the lowest tonic of its scale. It is also called the mandra.

mandra sadhana is the vocal training that involves a series of exercises in the mandra region of the scale. This exercise gives body and resonance to the voice.

manduka sabdam is a musical composition used in dance. Based on the story of 'Gajendra Moksham' the jatis mimic the musical equivalents of the croaking of frogs.

mangalam is a song of welcome and salutation. It is the concluding section of Carnatic concerts of dance and opera. It is mostly in the kirtana form and consists of a pallavi and several charanas which are sung in the same tune. The mangala gana signifies an auspicious moment.

mangala raga(s) are those ragas that are associated with auspiciousness. Mangalams are usually composed in these ragas. Dhanyasi, Asaveri, Vasanta and Yadukulakambhoji are some of the mangala ragas in the Carnatic tradition.

mani are the little beads threaded upon the strings of the tanpura which are used to fine-tune the swara.

Mani Ayyar, Madurai (1912–1968) was one of the greatest musicians of the Carnatic tradition. His father was Ramaswamy Ayyar, the older brother of another well-known singer, Pushpavanam Ayyar. Mani Ayyar trained in his early years with Rajam Bhagavatar and later under Haikesanallur Muthaiya Bhagavatar. He was a prodigy and began singing in public by his twelfth year. His shruti was extraordinarily pure and his fame lay principally in his repertoire of kritis and his distinctive technique of singing kalpana swaras. He was extremely popular during his lifetime and trained many students whose distinctive approach to swaras mark their style to this day.

Mani Ayyar, T.S. Pal-ghat was born in 1912. He was a mridangam player of rare distinction who had become an established artist even before he was twenty years old. He was the son of T.R. Seshabagavatar and was given the name of Amaswamy. Later he came to be known as Mani. He was first taught by Sitapuram Subbayyar, and then by Vasanta Ayyar. He started his musical career with performances in the Hari Katha concerts of Mukkai Sivaramakrishna Bhagavatar and went on to accompany musicians like Venkarma Bhagavatar. Later he came under the influence of the legendary Chembai Vaidyanatha Bhagavatar, who groomed him in a particular fashion which gave his mridangam playing a unique distinction of tone and an elegance of intonation. It was Chembai who introduced Mani Ayyar to the Madras audience in 1924 at the Jagannatha Bhakta

Sabha. At the age of fifteen, Mani Ayyar went to Tanjore and there he trained under the well-known mridangam vidwan, Tanjore Vaidyanathan. Here he was taught several of those touches of mridangam which over the years Mani Ayyar incorporated into one of the most attractive mridangam techniques of his time. Mani Ayyar's phrasing and mathematical accuracy became legendary over the years and he trained many students. The foremost of his students is Umayalpuram K. Sivaraman.

Manipravala kriti is a composition in which the lyrics use two or more languages but despite this remain gramatically accurate. Linguists usually compose Manipravala kritis. The kriti in Raga Bhairavi, *'Ni sari samaana'* and *'Thyagaraja Swami'* in Vachaspati are Manipravala kritis.

Manipuri is one of the six classical dance forms of India. The other five are Bharata Natyam, Kuchipudi, Odissi, Kathakali and Kathak.

Manjh is a Hindustani raga which is a mixture of Mand, Khamaj and Bilawal ragas. A well-known composition in this raga is *'Bahut bahut din pacche'* in Ektala.

Manjira is a raga mentioned in the *Brihaddharma Purana*. It is a raga derived from one of the six primary ragas named Gandhara. It also denotes the anklet full of little bells worn by dancers. Or the tinkling nupuram worn around the feet. It could also be the small saucer-shaped cymbals used to keep rhythm while singing bhajans or folk music.

Mannargudi is a town in the district of Thanjavur which is famous for its temple to Rajagopalaswamy. MUTHUSWAMI

DIKSHITAR'S well-known kriti *'Shri Rajagopala'* in the Raga Saveri was composed in praise of this deity.

manodharma sangeeta is music sung extempore— a product of the moment. It has particular significance in Carnatic music in which music composed by the great saints constitutes the basic element of music. In Hindustani classical music, since the compositions that are sung, known as bandishes, are short two or three movement pieces, almost all classical music is largely manodharma. The alap, the taans, the pallavi exposition, swara alapanas and the niraval are manodharma in Carnatic music. In Hindustani music even the composition has a touch of manodharma each time it is sung. Composing a kriti or a khayal does not constitute manodharma although it is creative and original. Manodharma is improvisational and is produced instantaneously without planning or forethought.

mantra is a short phrase or group of letters of the Sanskrit language purified by constant reiteration in the mind, thereby gaining a curious power and impulse. Mantra is derived from the word 'manan', meaning the constant repetition of thought in the mind. Magical properties are assigned to a mantra such as those of purifying the mind, entering it and stilling it. The gurumantra is the ceremonial giving of a set of Sanskrit syllables from the guru to the shishya. When these syllables are repeated, it is believed to trigger the mind with a new awareness.

marga means ancient as against DESI which is provincial and local, belonging to the region. A strict sense of rules is the characteristic of marga, while desi makes local adaptations of the rules. Thus there are marga and desi ragas and talas.

marga kriya is the marga technique of reckoning musical time.

marimba is a percussion instrument of African origin. A deeper toned xylophone with wooden slabs, it is played with a soft-headed stick. Darius Milhaus, the French composer, created concerts using the marimba and the vibraphone.

markata taan is a kind of taan that has the gait of a monkey. The movement of taans are often likened to the gait of animals like the elephant, peacock or snake. For instance, a taan is often said to be lumbering like a bear or jerky and unplanned like a frog.

marriage songs are of several kinds and exist for each linguistic group across the country. Among the many rituals associated with the nuptial ceremony, songs are among the most important. These are usually in the light ragas like Mand, Desh, Kaushika, Saindhavai, Mangala or Kaisiki. Songs welcoming the groom and his party are called Lali Sopana, Nalanga, Unjal. Each of these indicate a particular style of rhythm and expression.

Marva is a thaat in Hindustani music that corresponds to the fifty-third melakarta, Gamansrama.

masaka titti is a kind of bagpipe that gives a single drone note. It is associated with roving bands of storytellers. They use this instrument as a background drone to their chant-like storytelling. They blow into the air bag which, when it is filled with air, is then pressed with the hand, which lets the air escape through air holes at a slow pace, producing a steady sound. The storyteller continues to sing through the time the air is escaping.

Masit Khan was Tansen's son Vilas Khan's son. He was the first person to use dhrupad style's vilambit and gats for instrumental music, incorporating its use in playing the sitar and the sarod. Later the style came to be used for all kinds of instrumental renditions. The vilambit laya of dhrupad used for instrumental music also came to be called Delhi baj.

masitkhani is a particular kind of composition or gat on the sitar. It is attributed to Masit Khan, whose son is supposed to have been part of the court of Wajid Ali Shah. (See BAJ.)

Matanga is the author of the *Brihaddesa* of the fifth century. This is among the most authoritative sources on Indian music, containing vital material on ragas and jatis. Matanga is believed to be the originator of the raga system of Indian music. The lakshanakaras quote him widely. (See BRIHADDESA PURANA.)

matla is the name given to the first couplet of an Urdu ghazal.

matra is a unit of time measure and is used as the basic unit of the 108 talas of Indian music. (See TALA.)

matth is the name given to a school of thought. It is associated with an approach to raga and a set of beliefs attached to that style of singing a raga. There were several schools of thought or matths in ancient India although nobody can precisely say what these matths meant in actual physical terms. There is the Narada matth, the Shiva matth, the Hanuman matth, the Krishna matth and so on. Some ragas today bear the names of some of these matths and might be associated with this kind of inspiration manifested in, for example, Shivmat Bhairav, Shivmat Bhimpalasi, Hanumat Todi and so on. The Narada matth is associated with Carnatic music and the Hanuman matth with the Hindustani tradition.

mavu is the name given to the paste of rice and water which is applied to the mridangam's left side to dampen the vibrations and give the sound tone and timbre. The quantity and spread of the paste is adjusted so that the sound emitted is about an octave or the panchama below the note played on the right side of the mridangam.

Mayamalavagaula is the fifteenth melakarta. Malavagaula was its earlier name and Maya was added to it later to conform to the Kattapadi formula. The fact that this is a SAMPOORNA raga and has symmetrical tetrachords makes it the basic raga in learning Carnatic music. All the first alankaras are fashioned in this raga. Its Hindustani equivalent is Bhairav.

mayuri is the peacock-headed resonator played with a bow. It has a low serene tone.

medini prabandha belongs to the medieval period and uses all the six angas of the prabandha form—swara, piruda, pada, tenaka, tala and pata.

meend is a smooth uninterrupted glide from one note to another. Its closest equivalent in Western music is the portamento of bowed instruments.

Meera was one of the most mystic of saint poetesses of India. She lived in Rajasthan. Her songs adoring Krishna are sung throughout the country to this day. The raga Mirabai ki Malhar is named after her.

mehfil is chamber music. It is a close gathering of

people of similar mind who assemble to listen to music. It also used to be called bazm.

mela (melakarta) means a parent scale of notes possessing a definise melodic character, with each note bearing a particular relationship to a tonic note and retaining that characteristic in ascent and descent. A full complement of seven notes are used in both the ascending and descending scales. There are seventy-two melakartas emerging from the twelve notes of a full scale. This then becomes the basis from which a raga is derived. The character of a mela is so clear that the shortest section of its ascending or descending notes reveals the identity of the mela to the listener. Its Hindustani equivalent is the THAAT. The melas are seventy-two in number and the thaats are ten in number. The ragas are formed out of these melas

as melodic units from which ragas are born. (See JANAKA.)

melakarta ragas are melakarta scales which can be made into a raga. Unlike in Western classical music, a scale is only the substance from which a raga is then made. Hari Kambhoji and Karaharapriya are examples.

mela nomenclature is the system of naming the 72 melakartas.

membranophone is the instrument that uses a membrane to produce a musical sound. A drum would be a membranophone. It is also called avanuddha vadya.

meru is the fret nearest the peg area of the veena.

merukhand is formed of the two words, 'meru' and 'khand'. Meru literally means the spine and khand is a section or a part. Merukhand exploits the mathematical relationship between consonant and dissonant notes on the scale in all its relationships, making it possible to produce 5040 varieties of distinctive taan arrangements. The *Sangita Ratnakara* of Sarangdeva discusses merukhand at length.

Meruswamy was one of the samasthana vidwans who lived in the court of the Sarabhoji. Often referred to by the name of Kokila Katha Meru Swami, his bird-like clarity of voice gave him great power as a Harikatha performer.

Mian ki Malhar is a raga of Hindustani music associated with Tansen. It is a raga of the rains.

Mian ki Todi also of Tansen's making, is a morning raga.

minor tone is a shruti with a frequency of about 10/9. The interval between the chatushruti rishabha and the antara gandhara is a minor tonic.

mirasee refers to the inheritence of a musician whether through his family, place or any other source.

misra refers to a kind of classification of nada. Umapatam by Umapati lists three heads: sajiva, which is music sung by the human voice, nirjiva or music of an instrument such as the veena or sitar, and misra which is the sound of the flute or shehnai where the prana or wind is blown by the player. The animate or inanimate origin of sound is at the foundation of this concept. Haripala in the *Sangeeta Sudhakara* uses the terms chetana, achetana and misra for the same divisions. Terms like prani sambhava, aprani sambhava and ubhaya also mean the same thing.

misrab is the wire plectrum with which stringed instruments are plucked. This is usually made of copper or steel.

misra raga really means those compound ragas which are usually two ragas joined together. There are several styles of mixing ragas. The poorvanga of one raga with the uttaranga of the other is one way of effecting this. The real test of a mishra raga is in the way the two ragas mesh into each other. This requires skill and intellect in the musician.

misra taan See CHAKRA TAAN.

misra tala is a compound of different talas.

modal shift occurs when the shadja or the tonic note is shifted, producing another raga. This is called GRIHA BHEDA in Indian music.

mode is the Greek and ecclesiastical scale. The major mode would be the Shankarabharanam scale which is the Bilawal scale of Hindustani music.

modulation refers to a change of key in Western music. Such shifts let the composer use parallel and consonant keys, helping the vertical parts of a composition come about.

Mohamed Shah Rangila was a Mughal ruler of the eighteenth century who was an ardent musician and a patron of music. The composer named SADARANG, whose name is insinuated into his compositions, has dedicated many of his compositions to Mohamed Shah.

mohara is the concluding seal of a performance, sometimes done three times like a Hindustani TIHAYI. It is usually done in rhythmic display. The finish then feels conclusive and final.

moorcchhana/murcchhanas are the scales that emerge when each successive note of the scale is made the tonic note and a set of notes become the scale from that point. It is the name given to the scales derived from the Sa grama, the Ga grama and the Ma grama by the method of the modal shift. The word is derived from the root 'moorcch' meaning unconscious or subconscious. For example, *Sa, Ri, Ga, Ma, Pa, Dha, Ni, Sa* becomes, in its next murcchhana, *Ri, Ga, Ma, Pa, Dha, Ni, Sa, Ri,* and the next becomes *Ga, Ma, Pa, Dha, Ni, Sa, Ri, Ga,* and so on right on to the nishad of the scale. It implies an awareness of the differing pathways a raga takes in its passage. The change of the shadja in emphasising a note gives the mind an opportunity to take another pathway in the raga which changes the feel of the first raga that was being performed. When ragas are derived from moorchhanas the technique is called moorchhana paddhati. (See also PANCHADASA.)

moorchhanakaraka raga is a raga from which several moorchhanas emerge like Bhairavi and Malhar.

morsing (moorsing) is a thin flat iron slip called the tongue attached to a ring-shaped circular metal passing across the centre of the ring and sticking out just a little. The instrument is held in the mouth and struck with the forefinger which makes the metal tongue vibrate, making the mouth act as a resonator. This instrument plays laya and jati sequences along with the mridangam. The moorsing can be made to approximate the scale of the singer by using a little wax at the tip of the tongue. This instrument is also called JEW'S HARP.

mridangam is the classical two-faced drum used as percussion in Carnatic music, and played horizontally with the two hands by laying it on the lap. Mridangam literally means 'made of clay'. It is made out of a scooped out single block of wood, usually a neem tree or jack or coconut. The two skin tympani on the two sides are dampened by a smooth paste of rice and water on the left side and a black dampener made of iron dust and rice on the right. In the hands of a good player, the mridangam could sound like a human voice, rich and tempered, and has a calling intonation which in temple and kacheri, is very evocative.

mudra is a name introduced in the lyric of a song or kriti which identifies either the composer by name or his nom de plume, the raga, the tala or the type of composition.

mughane   mughaneya means a piece of music in Persian originating from the word naghma. The mughane is male and mughaneya is female.

mukhavina is a wind instrument like a small nagaswaram.

mukhra literally means face and applies to the face or the upper part of the right half (DAYAN) of the tabla. It also refers to the first few words of a composition leading on to its sam. This phrase is naturally used every time the avarta is over. It is the phrase by which a composition is recognised. It is found in all kinds of compositions—the bhajan, the thumri and the khayal. It is also called the muh. Well-known compositions are referred to by their mukhras.

mukhyang is the most important part/phrase of a raga that gives the raga its particular identity. It is also called the PAKAR, which means 'to hold'. It is thus the phrase that helps provide a grip on the raga.

murki is a short sharp figure of two or three notes

so uttered that it occurs within the space of a half matra. This figure has decorative power and is also known as phanda or gitkari.

Mushtaq Husein Khan (1872–1964) was a musician of the Rampur-Saheswan gharana. His voice was big and resonant and he had an enormous collection of bandishes and other compositions in his inheritence.

Muthuswamy Dikshitar (1776–1835) was the youngest of the great Carnatic trinity. Born in Tiruvarur in the constellation of Kartika, he studied music under his father Ramaswamy Dikshitar and his mother Subbalakshmi Ammal. He went to Benares where he stayed for five years. He was impressed by the dhrupad style in Hindustani music which influenced his approach to his own compositions. He was a prolific composer in Sanskrit. He used the vilambit tempo in his many compositions, which are full of subtle gamakas and graces.

N

na is the mnemonical name for the first shruti of the three types of nishada used in the 72 melakarta categorization. It is the same as the shuddha nishada.

nabhi swara is a kind of vocal production that is layered with harmonics and seems to originate at the navel of the singer.

nada is an emanation of the life principle or prana. It is the basic vibration that enters the audio level and can be heard as sound as it impinges on the consciousness. It is the matrix of sound before its differentiation as swara and note. It is a mystical concept. It has several connotations, one of which is the nada brahma, which is an esoteric understanding of the silence of the spheres, a sound to hear which you have to listen within. This concept has held the imagination of Indian classical music for millenia and continues to inform thinking on music even now. Its subdivisions include the AHATA, which is the heard sound, and the ANAHATA, which is the unheard sound.

nadamaya is the form of the raga experienced through the swara, its shrutis through its alap and the composition and its many variations through tala, laya and layakaris. The devamaya, in contrast, is the visual representation of the raga as a picture, bringing out its gait, raga rasa and tempi.

Nadanamakriya is a janya of the fifteenth melakarta, Mayamalavagaula. There is no Hindustani raga of this name. If Bhairav is sung from the madhyam swara it sounds like this raga.

nada rupa is the embodied form of nada. In the kriti in Kalyani 'Nammi vachana nannu', Thyagaraja described the nada rupa as God.

nadaswaram (See NAGA-SWARAM.)

nadatma rupa is the same as nadamaya and devatma rupa is the same as devamaya mentioned earlier. Nadatma rupa is the sound picture of the raga which is its aural form while the devatma is the visual form of the raga as drawn in the raga-ragini pictures of ragas.

nadayog is the work on the swara as a kind of yoga where the swara is understood to be fundamental and the raga is secondary.

nadayogi is a musician who practices music as part of yoga, a kind of rigorous discipline that gathers all the human faculties into the art. Thyagaraja was supposed to have been the nadayogi of Carnatic music as Tansen was of Hindustani music.

nadopasana is the practice of nada as a meditative exercise that cleanses musical perceptions.

nadopasika is one who meditates on the swaras of music and obtains the power of nada from the exercise.

nadotpatti is the origin of nada. Sarangadeva describes this origin of nada by saying that the soul or the atma, wanting to express itself, stirs the mind, striking the fire in the body. This moves the wind, which reverberates against the navel, the heart and the vocal chords in an upward path, producing nada. This is described in Thyagaraja's composition the charana of which begins 'Moksha mugalada' in Raga Saramati, 'da' denoting fire and 'na' denoting prana.

nagada is a martial drum played with sticks and accompanies the shehnai.

nagapasam is a crescent-shaped metal piece that is attached to the top of the bowl of the veena. Its other name is mooladharama. It keeps the tension of the strings of the veena steady and secure. The veena's seven strings are held by this nagapasam.

Nagapattanam is a coastal city in the district of Thanjavur. There is a Shiva temple and a Vishnu temple in this town and the Carnatic music trinity is said to have visited this temple and sung songs in praise of the dieties of the temple. Thyagaraja's Toḍi raga kriti beginning 'Evaru taliyaka' and 'Karmane balwanta' in Saveri are dedicated to this temple. Syama Shastri's 'Nilaya-takshi' in Phanaz raga and Muthuswamy Dikshitar's

'Amba nilayakshi' and 'Soundara raja' in Nilambari and Brindavani also address these deities.

nagara is a large hemispherical drum consisting of copper bodies bound by hide at the ends. It is played in temples. It is carried on a carriage pulled by a man between the shafts and follows the deity in procession. Elephants also help draw the carriage in some temples.

Nagaraja Rao was a well-known flute player of this century who was born in Kumbakonam. A student of the famous Surabha Sastri, speed, clarity and power were the chief characteristics of his style.

nagaswaram is among the most popular Carnatic instruments. It is an instrument of celebration and auspiciousness. It is believed to be about 800 years old. The right name of the instrument is nagaswaram and not nadaswaram which was a way of pronouncing the word in the thirties of this century. It is a wood wind instrument, conical in shape, made of a kind of ebony. Nagaswarams are also made of soapstone. It is a reed instrument and has five finger stop holes. Its pitch is loud and is at its best in the open air.

naghma is used to denote any piece of music.

Naghmat-e-Asaphi was a work on music written in 1813 by Mohamed Raza, a native of Patna. This book mentions for the first time that the Bilawal scale is the shuddha scale of Hindustani music. It was the Kafi thaat which was considered to be the shuddha scale until his time.

nalika murali is a kind of flute devised by Professor Sambamurty, one of the well-known musicologists of this century. It has a plastic tube into which air is blown. It is so con-structed that even a novice is able to produce rich tones on the flute which makes it easier to learn.

nalla tarana is an organ-like instrument. It has nineteen pipes played with the help of bellows and the pipe mouth is opened with a key attached to a keyboard. It produces a reedy sound.

Namadeva was a saint whose abhangs are still widely popular.

nama sankirtanam is a musical composition used for religious purposes. It is used in congregation and traces its roots to the *Bhagavatam Namavali* or a recitation of god's name.

namavali is a string of names of the Gods used as part of bhajans and katha kalakshepams. In cycles of one or two or even three avartas, the concept of the song is clearly brought out. The sheer volume of congregational singing produces a deep impact on the mind. Most of these namavalis are composed in adi tala.

Nandanar is among the sixty-three Shaivaite saints and the main protagonist of the famous *Nandanar Charitram.* Nandanar is reputed to have lived more than two thousand years ago and was associated with several miraculous happenings in his life.

Nandi Bharatam is the name of the last section of the *Bharata Natya Shastra.*

Nandikeswara is the author of the grantha entitled *Abhinaya Darpana.* It is a standard work on dance and is quoted as an authority.

Nannu Mian was one of the greatest performers of the dholak. He was greatly admired by his contemporaries. Musicians like Mridangam Narayana Swami Appa held him in great esteem. His brother Chhotu Mian and he were samasthana vidwans of the state of Pudukottai. Nannu Mian's name went down in history because of a contest between him and Somu Bhagavatar of Talainagar, which produced the pallavi in Saveri raga, '*Saveri biri rani palukurt*'.

napumsaka raga is a raga without a gender. Narada in his *Sangita Makaranda* described ragas of three kinds— purusha which is male, sthri which is female and napumsaka or neuter.

nar awaz is the voice of a male. It generally relates to a rich carrying baritone.

Narada is one of the most commonly occurring characters in the history of music. There is the Narada of the epics, the musician of the Gods, a sage and a player of the veena who gave gnyana as his special gift. He was also the figure who is reported to have inspired Valmiki to write his

Ramayana. Then there is Narada, the author of the *Grantha Narada Siksha.* Written in Sanskrit about two thousand years ago, the gandhara grama is fully described in this grantha. Then there is another Narada, the author of the *Sangita Makaranda* which describes the gender classification of ragas. (See NAPUMSAKA RAGA.) The classification of ragas, as muktanga kampita, ardha kampita, and kampa vihina have also been described in this grantha. Thyagaraja had apparently studied Narada's *Sangita Makaranda,* as references to it exist in his composition to Narada. Kritis such as *'Narada guruswamy'* in Raga Darbar and the song *'Sri Narada mune gururaya'* in Raga Bhairavi are mentioned as having been blessed by Narada.

Narada matth is the 'matth' or school of music founded by Narada. There are other matths like Hanuman matth, Shiva matth and Someswara matth. (See MATTH)

nat means actor or one who forms part of a dance or drama troupe.

Nata is a janya raga derived from the thirty-sixth mela, Chalanta.

Nataraja literally means the King of Dancers and is the name by which the famous deity at the temple of Chidambaram is known. The bronze statue of the timeless pose of the dancing Shiva in the temple at Chidambaram has become the symbol of the dance of the cosmic order.

Nathabhairavi is the name of the twentieth melakarta.

nathna means the nostril. In musical lore the word stands for the quality of nasal resonance that makes the voice rich.

natya dharma is the code of ethics to be observed by a dancer. These have been placed under four heads: dharma pertaining to the dancer; dharma pertaining to the accompanying musician, instrumentalists and singers; dharma pertaining to the organisers and dharma pertaining to the audience.

Natya Shastra is the fifth century document written by Bharata Muni. It sets down the basic foundations for the Indian performing arts, particularly Indian dance and its techniques. This book has 32 major sections. The book also covers the field of music and is considered among the most important basic documents on the performing arts. There are three sections on music and the rest is on dance. The *Natya Shastra* is often referred to as the fifth Veda.

naubat is the term given to a performance by a group of musicians, nine in number, playing both string and wind instruments. The performers sit on the arches of gateways to cities or on balconies in palaces or mausoleums. In some places the naubat is performed at certain set times which indicate to people the time of day. Emperor Akbar is said to have played in the naubat.

Nauka Charitram is one of the most popular of Thyagaraja's operas. The story of *Nauka Charitram* was of Thyagaraja's own invention and is not drawn from the Puranas. The whole opera is in Telugu except for the *phala shruti* at the beginning which is in Sanskrit and which is a benediction. In the 'Prahalada Bhakti Vijayam' section of the opera there are some Sanskrit shlokas. Thyagaraja also made sure that in his operas the opening and the closing songs were in the same raga. Except for one ghana raga, Varali, the rest of the ragas used in the opera are nakti ragas.

nava graha kirtanas are a group of songs composed by Muthuswamy Dikshitar to the nine planets of the zodiac. These are also referred to as the vara kirtanas which are songs for each day of the week. Beginning on Sunday, the kirtanas for the days of the week are composed in the following ragas: Saurashtra, Asaveri, Surati, Natakurunji, Athana, Pharaz and Yadukula Kambhoji. The two points of the ecliptic are known as Rahu and Ketu or Dragon's head and Tail. Rahu is in Raga Ramamanohari and Ketu in Chamara raga.

navaragamalika are the nine kritis of Syama Shastri in praise of the goddess Meenakshi of the temple of Madurai.

navarasa are the nine types of emotional colouring. These include shringara which is love, hasya which is merriment or laughter, karuna which is compassion, raudra which is anger or ferocity, vira which is heroism, bhayankara which is terror, bibhatsa which is disgust, adbhuta which is wonder and shanta which is serenity or tranquillity. There are also two other rasas which have been added on to the list above in later years. These are bhakti, which is devotion and vatsalya, which is tenderness.

navaratnamala is a garland of nine kirtanas composed by Swati Tirunal on the theme of bhakti. There are nine kinds of bhakti which are sravanam, through attentive listening, kirtanam, singing religious songs, smaranam, mentally imagining the deity, padasevanam, worship at the feet of the deity, archanam, making an offering, vandanam, paying respects, dasyam or service of the deity, sakhyam or constant companionship of the deity in the mind and atmanivedanam or self enquiry.

navaratri kirtana is a song composed by Swati Tirunal. There are several of these and are intended to be sung during the Navaratri festival. The ragas follow the sequence Sankarabharanam, Kalyani, Saveri, Todi, Bhairavi, Pantuvarali, Suddha Saveri, Natakurunji and Arabhi.

navavarna kirtanas are the nine compositions of Muthuswamy Dikshitar in praise of the deity Kamalamba of Tiruvarur temple. The nine are in the sequence: Todi, Anandabhairavi, Kalyani, Sankarabharanam, Kambhoji, Bhairavi, Punnagavarali, Sahana, Ghanta, Ahiri and Sri. Todi is a dhyana kirtana and Sri is a mangala kirtana.

Nasrul geeti are the songs composed by tne Bengali poet Kazi Nasrul Islam.

nayak has martial connotations and means a leader in any group of musicians.

nibaddha is a composition that is set to a tala. The raga is not fully born until it becomes nibaddha, complete with metrical gait, and when sung has words to explore its inner reaches. The design for growth is provided by the alap, swara vistar, taans and boltaans, each directed towards explicating the raga and the composition. The ANIBADDHA is the unbounded area of alapana and swara prasthara where there is no tala which confines the infinity of the raga, giving it a shape and architecture.

nija sangita means music that is true and unspoilt.

nindastuti kirtanas are kirtanas composed around the stories of gods and goddesses whose faults are highlighted as an indirect act of adoration. Thyagaraja's Athana raga composition that begins '*Illalo pranatarthi*' is one such composition.

nipun (naipunya) is a level of skill which is natural. It is an unguarded ease and perfection in the execution of music.

nirgita is a composition that has no words but the sargam syllables alone. The jatis belong in this genre.

nirgun literally means without attributes. This is a characteristic approach to life popularised by the saint Kabir who approaches God as formless and without any attributes describable in words. Kabir and his followers who are called Kabir Panthees, propagated this approach to God and creation as a manifestation of this One without parts.

nishada is the seventh note of the scale.

nissabdha kriya is the act of reckoning rhythm without sound.

niyama are the rules that govern the execution and grasp of ragas and the methods of their expression like swara, shruti, laya and the rules of vadi and samavadi. There are several mandatory rules and some that have the quality of discrimination. Tala niyama are the laws of tala that control a composition. Sahitya niyama are the rules that pertain to the values of the literary and linguistic content of compositions. Chhand niyama are the rules of prosody of the lyrical structure of the composition. Prabandha niyama are the rules relating to the compositions themselves, like a chaturang or geet or khayal or dhrupad with their respective inevitable structural compulsions. Ganakala niyamas are the rules that pertain to the time when ragas should be sung, like Yaman in the evening or Bhairav at dawn. Then there are niyamas related to appropriateness of themes of compositions. For example vairagya themes or themes that direct attention to the perishability of life should not be sung at the time of marriage. Kalpana swaraniyama are the rules related to the performance of sargams. This would entail beginning with short pieces and then lengthening them as the series develops. Sadhaka niyamas are the rules related to the sadhana of music and time duration, nature of dhyana during sadhana and breath control.

nohar (nauhar) vani is a Rajput vani of dhrupad. This belonged in the family of Shrichand. This was a very popular vani in Rajasthan.

nom tom is the kind of alap that uses the syllables *nom tom* to elaborate the raga. Dhrupad singers use this kind of alap very frequently. Some khayal singers are also notable for this style of singing.

nritya is the section of a performance where pure dance is presented, complete with a display of footwork, technical skills and abhinaya.

nyasa swara is the final note of an alapana or the note on which the phrase will rest. In the olden days this note was established for each song. Traditionally there were twenty-one positions on the scale in which a song could end.

O

Om is the sound in Hindu cosmology believed to be the pervading silence of the universe. It represents in the Hindu system the Absolute as sound and is often called nada brahma. The production of this sound by the human voice is the totality of all perceived vibrations whether by the ear or by the subtle senses of the spirit.

Om Ananta Hari is the basic syllable of the mantra on which dhrupad alap is based. It is believed to inspire those subtle vibrations that kindle music in the mind.

Onkarnath Thakur was the disciple of Pandit Vishnu Digambar Palusker (1897-1967). He had a high pitched tenor with a rich bloom to it. His music was highly emotional and dramatic in its expression. He was the Dean of the Music Faculty of Benares Hindu University. He wrote the *Sangeetanjali* and *Pranava Bharati*, two musical texts and several compositions using Pranava Rang as his signature. Dr N. Rajam, the violinist, is one of his most distinguished shishyas as also Balwant Rai Bhatt and P.N.Barwe.

P

padam or pada is a poetic composition with verses of lyrics. Each verse is scored to music and sung in elaboration of one raga or a series of ragas as in raga malikas. Padams can be both sung or danced.

Pahadi is a favourite raga in Maharashtra stage music. It belongs to the Bilawal thaat (Dhira Sankarabharanam). There is no raga that is similar to Pahadi in Carnatic music.

pakad is a set of note figures that gives an instant clue to the raga. It literally means to hold or grip. The same pakad is never repeated in another raga.

pakhawaj is a cylindrical two-faced drum which accompanies been and dhrupad performances.

palta is a swara figure describing a raga's geometry. These figures can be complex or simple but their geometrical shape varies and their rendering reveals the virtuosity of a musician's imagination.

pallavi in Carnatic music is the basic first movement. In the Hindustani system it is called the STHAYI.

panchama is the fifth note of the scale. It is an ACHALA SWARA and in any given scale does not have a sharp or flat variation. It is a note that traditionally is believed to be the sound of the Indian koel.

paran denotes mnemonics for double, triple, thirds and fifths of a tempo in tala cycles. There are several kinds of parans—Gat-paran, Chalradar, Farmaishi and so on, with geometric characteristics.

Patiala gharana is a Punjab gharana. It has

shades of the Gwalior gharana in its inspiration. Originally it was started by a family of musicians from Kasur, a small area near Lahore, who served in the court of the Maharaja´ of Patiala. Fateh Ali and Ali Baksh, Kale Khan Mian Jad, Bade Gulam Ali Khan, Akhtar Husein and Ashiq Ali Khan were among the gharana's principal mentors. Powerful enunciation, purity and transparency of swara and a subtle spiritual exultation are the principal characteristics of this gharana. Its taans and swara figures have a special appeal to the young. Its present notable incumbents are Ajoy Chakravarty, Raza Ali Khan and Abdul Aziz.

peshkar is an Urdu word that means introduction to a tala. It is the first and simplest expression used to introduce the tala. Thereafter the various other elements of tabla playing are brought in, like the bol, gat, paran, rela and so on. It has connotations in dance too where the tala in Kathak is used to introduce the first steps of a dancer on the stage.

phaag are the songs of the Holi festival coming in the month of March or Phagun.

phanda (See MURKI.)

Pilu belongs to the Kafi thaat (Karaharapriya melakarta). Raga Kirwani in Carnatic music bears a resemblance to Pilu.

pluta is one of the seven tala notations in Carnatic music used to explicate the matra with signs.

poorab baz is the term for the style of tabla-playing characteristic of eastern Uttar Pradesh. The region includes Farrakabad, Benares and Lucknow. The special characteristics of this style are: (i) Benares is a style of playing the tabla with splayed fingers. The left drum is slightly tilted to the right and so the *dha* sounds close to the sound *gha*.

(ii) Farrakabad is a style which has several tempo variations. It is decorous and has special value for dance.

(iii) Lucknow resembles the style of Delhi and has a particularly sharp slapping sound that is distinctive of this school.

poorvang is the lower tetrachord of the scale with a range from the shadja to madhyama.

prabandha is a composition predating dhrupads. It is a completely composed piece of music tied in completely with regard to tala structure, metre, beginning, middle and conclusion. Its rhythmic system is completely enunciated in the composition, its raga is clear, unambiguous and complete. Any kind of song based on these factors will be a prabandha. The pra-bandha of the *Geet Govinda* of Jaideva is a case in point, where the musical structure has a certain formality which is its characteristic.

prahar is approximately three hours of time. It relates to the time of ragas and the periods of performance. This division of the day is related to the concept of the inner rotation within the human body in step with the diurnal and nocturnal rotation of the earth.

pratyanga is descriptive of various specified parts of the body in dance such as bahu (arms), udar (stomach), manibandha (waist) etc. It also applies to ragas where ragas are understood to be living entities with angas like poorva anga and uttaranga or the two tetrachords.

prayoga is a technique of expression in raga, a characteristic progression, a manner of negotiation on the scale.

Pundarik Vittal was among the great musicologists of the South. In around 1598 he wrote several granthas like *Ragamala, Raga Manjari* and *Nritya Nirnaya.*

Prana Piya was the pen name of Ustad Vilayat Khan of the Agra gharana.

Q

Qawwal Bacche were the musicians who sang in the qawwali style. The legendary Hazrat Amir Khusro was an ardent follower of the Qawwal Bacche inheritence.

qawwali originated from the root 'qual' which were the mystical sayings of Sufi saints. It is believed that the qawwali form of music became popular in the thirteenth century. Qawwalis were sung by men who were followers of the Khwaja Moinuddin Chishti Garib Nawaz. He belonged to Ajmer in Rajasthan and his followers were known as Qawwal Bacche. These men realized the power of using Hindustani classical music to popularize the words of saints. Sufism made deep inroads into the Indian consciousness through the power of music. All the technical elements of Hindustani classical music can be found in the singing of the qawwali. The taans and the sargams, the meends and the bol development are all part of the techniques of classical music. The khayal form of music originated from these sources of the qawwal.

R

raas is the music of the Brij tradition connected with Radha, Krishna and the gopis.

raga constitutes the basis of the music of the subcontinent. A raga is neither a melody nor a mere scale, nor is it a mode. The principles on which a raga is built are as follows: A raga must have a minimum of five notes up and down the scale. It can have more notes—six or seven. But the minimum is five. The raga scale must have two pivotal points situated in each tetrachord. These notes are called VADI and SAMAVADI. The raga's motion is organised towards these notes. The raga also has a set of notes called PAKAD, which provide a grip on the raga. These are characteristic turns of phrase by which the raga's principal characteristic can be recognised. The concert of raga is unique to the Indian tradition and is common to both the Hindustani and the Carnatic traditions. As ragas are based on the human utterance of swara and not the instrumental tuning fork-based note, it becomes, in a sense, a living utterance. It is this quality of utterance that is the most appealing element of raga music.

ragamala literally means a garland of ragas. It is a composition in which several ragas come into life and retreat.

ragi are shabad kirtan singers of the Sikh religious tradition.

ragini is conceived as a female raga. Raginis are usually understood to be the wives of the ragas.

Raja Man Singh is one of

the legendary musical figures of Hindustani music. He was the Maharaja of Gwalior in the fifteenth century and was responsible for the preservation of dhrupad by patronising these singers and including them in the palace entourage. He was a singer himself and composed several dhrupads. His name is always included in the texts of the songs.

Rajab Ali Khan was a great khayal singer born in Narsingh Garh (1874–1959). He was the son of the sarangi player Moghul Khan. Ustad Rajab Ali Khan settled in the State of Dewas near Indore. Rajab Ali Khan's style was complex and his powerful choot taans became a legend in his own time. His students were Shankar Sarnaik and Ganesh Behra.

Ramkrishna Buwa Vaze was a well-known musician of the Gwalior gharana. He was given the title of Naveen Tansen. He died in 1945.

Rampur gharana is a branch of the Gwalior gharana. Many musicologists consider Wazir Khan Saheb, Amjad Ali Khan, Ravi Shankar, Ali Akbar and Hafiz Ali Khan part of the Rampur Senia gharana. It is one of the major gharanas of Hindustani music and Bhatkhande obtained a lot of reference material from the Rampur musicians for his celebrated seminal works on Hindustani music.

Rangile gharana is another name for the Agra gharana. It acquired this name because of the fact that its musicians were the descendants of singers at the court of Mohamed Shah Rangile.

rasika is a lover of music, also called rasia.

Raskhan was an Afghan Muslim who was a devoted Krishna bhakt and lived in

Brindawan. He composed several dohas in Brij bhasha on Lord Krishna which are sung to this day.

Rasoolan Bai was one of the greatest thumri singers of the Benares gharana, often called the Poorab ang. Her teacher was Shammu Khan.

Ratanjankar S.N. was a musicologist and singer and the disciple of Pandit V.N. Bhatkhande. He later became principal of the Morris College of Music in Lucknow. He was the first adviser to the committee that was constituted to grade classical musicians for the All India Radio. He discovered a new raga called Salakvarali. He died on 13 February 1974, the same day that Ustad Amir Khan passed away.

razakhani is a type of sitar-gat whose highly articulated strokes of the mirzab is its principal characteristic. A kind of accenting distinguishes the gat.

rela is among the technical flourishes of the tabla. It is used as a part of a tabla performance and is the style of doubling, quadrupling or playing in multiples of eight. The bols are such that it is possible to play such fractions. The bol that begins *dhatita dhidanaka dhathita dhida naka dhatatadhatita dhidanaka dhatata dhatita dhidanaka dhatir dhidanaka dhatata dhata dhatata dhidanaga*, is a rela.

rishabha is the second note of the scale of Indian music. Rishabha means bull. In the musical scale the Shadja which is the tonic note is the symbol of the creator-destroyer Lord Shiva. In Indian temples the bull named Nandi stands guard before the gate. The implication of confronting the bull before entering the temple is stretched to mean that it is only through the rishabha that you may approach Shiva, the Shadja.

Roshanara Begum was among the foremost singers of the Kirana gharana and was a disciple of Ustad Abdul Karim Khan. She moved to Pakistan after the partition of India. She was counted among the greats of Hindustani music.

rosin (See beroza.)

rudra veena is an instrument also called the BEEN. This consists of a large diameter hollow bamboo with two sounding bowls at its two ends. Its frets are fixed with wax to avoid damaging the bamboo. Rudra is the name of Lord Shiva. This veena has a rich tone and is among the most popular ancient instruments of India.

rupak tala is a tala in the Hindustani tradition that has seven matras. The first beat is the *sam*, the second beat is on the fourth matra and the third beat is on the sixth matra. The Carnatic rupaka tala has only six matras.

S

sabad are the songs of prayer in the Guru Granth Saheb, the Sikh scripture. When these songs are sung, the audience joins in creating a congregational kind of singing.

sabha gana denotes singing in a sabha or to a large audience, not an intimate mehfil.

Sabrang was the signature used in the compositions of the Patiala maestro, Ustad Bade Gulam Ali Khan.

Sadarang was one of the principal musicians and composers at the court of the Mughal king Mohamed Shah (1719-1740). His official name was Niyamat Khan, but he was called Sadarang by the Mughal king. His compositions had colour and beauty and he became highly popular in his time. His compositions are sung to this day. (See also ADARANG.)

sadhana is a word commonly used to indicate practice and is popularly misused in this sense. Sadhana is directed towards a spiritual objective, and uses music as a medium to transform the inner nature of the musician so that after a prolonged period of sadhana the musician's art has a power that seems incalculable. While practice in the ordinary sense is a mechanical exercise, sadhana is a creative endeavour.

sadra is a khayal composition in jhaptala. The word sadra is derived from the word 'sahdara' meaning three. It is symbolic of the three beats that represents the three entrances into the tala cycle. The jhaptala in which sadras are composed has three beats to a cycle.

Sain Karim was a well-known musician of the Sham Chaurasi gharana. He was grandfather of Ustad Salamat Ali Khan who lived in Pakistan. Sain Karim lived in the court of the Maharaja of Jammu and Kashmir. He had a sweet voice. In his last years he is said to have lost his mind.

sam is the first and the most important point of stress in a tala cycle. This position in the cycle gives a rhythmic quality of summation to the musical phrase. The tala cycle functions like a heart whose beats squeeze towards the sam and relax towards the unstressed beat called khali in a giant lup and dup of the heart's basic beat.

samasthana vidwan is a musician recognised by the royal court or a respected musical establishment.

sampoorna jati is a raga that has all the seven notes in it.

samvadi comes from the root 'vaad', which means to speak together or hold a dialogue. This is a note in the scale of a raga which is separated from the VADI by four or five notes. The samvadi's status in a raga is equal to that of the vadi.

sanchara literally means motion. In music it indicates a manner of exploration of the terrain of a raga with a particular gait, geometry, progression and rest.

sandhee prakash raga is the raga which is sung when dawn and dusk meet or when darkness and light meet. These ragas are intended to be sung at dawn or in the evening.

sangat means to accompany, be together.

sangeet is a term that has two parts: 'san' which is derived from 'sam' and 'geet'. 'Sam' means together and 'geet' means a

147

song. It also connotes material for singing.

Sangeet Darpan is a seventeenth century grantha written around 1625 by Damodar Mishra. It discusses ragas and raginis at length and is an authoritative source material.

Sangeet Makarand is a ninth century grantha. In this grantha the names of all the shrutis of the scale have different names to those known at that time. Here the twenty-one male, the twenty-four female and fourteen neuters of the ragas have been described. The concept of male and female ragas first came out of this grantha. The author, Narada, was perhaps the first to make the raga concept of Indian music a part of the psychological inheritence of the subcontinent.

Sangeet Parijat was written about 1750 by Pandit Ahobal. This book is basic in many ways and has for the first time used the length of the strings of a veena to pinpoint the various flat and sharp notes of the scale.

Sangeeta Ratnakara is a thirteenth century document authored by Sarangadeva. Hindustani music is based largely on this grantha. There are four major adhyayas or chapters in the first part to this book: Swaradhyay, Raga Vivekadhyay, Prabandhadhyay and Taladhyay. The second part of the grantha is divided into Vadyadhyay and Nartanadhyay. This grantha covers a wide area of scholarship and understanding and has influenced all writing and teaching of music since the days of Sarangadeva.

Sangeeta Saramrita was written by the Tanjore maharaja, Rao Bhonsle between 1763–68. This grantha, together with another called *Ragalakshan*, covered Carnatic music's 72 melakartas and janya ragas.

sangeet upasana means the devoted practice of music.

sankeerna (sankirna) raga is a compound of two ragas. The difference between sankeerna and chhayalagat ragas is that chhayalagat ragas have traces of other ragas whereas the sankeerna raga has the clear lineaments of two ragas.

santoor is a harp-like instrument played with both hands using sticks. It is believed to be a Kashmiri instrument. Its entrance into classical music is of recent origin. Its principal players are Pandit Shiv Kumar Sharma and Om Prakash Chaurasia. An increasing band of players have welcomed this instrument into the classical fold.

sapat taan is an arpeggio that shoots straight from its base note to the upper reaches of the scale at great speed.

saptak is the series of notes that forms the musical scale. This has seven notes and hence the name.

sarana are those resonating strings that run beneath the playing strings of the sitar. The strings are also called tarab. These are tuned to the notes of the scale and resonate when the playing string is played, giving the note a shine and a glitter. The sarangi, the surbahar, the esraj and the vichitra veena—all have these tarab strings.

Sarang Deva (1175–1247) was a musicologist who wrote the well-known book *Sangeeta Ratnakara*, the seminal text on music which for its time was completely non-controversial. The merukhand system has been fully explained in this text, giving the mathematical derivation of 5040 taans that form the seven notes of the scale.

sarangi is a bowed instrument and is a basic accompanying instrument in Hindustani music. Today this instrument is also played solo. It has twenty-seven strings and is fretless. Its sound is a close approximation of a human voice of the soprano range.

sargam is the practice of the names of the notes, constituting the solfa passages of the music. In several gharanas of music the sargams are highly developed in complexity and skill. The Patiala gayaki and the Bhendi Bazar gharana, all use a large part of a concert to sing sargams.

sarod is one of the most popular concert instruments of today. The word has come from the Persian 'sarood' meaning sweet. It is a variant of the rabab and its present shape has a metal plate fitted across the instrument's belly. The sarod has steel strings while the rabab, its ancestor, had gut strings. It is played with a plectrum.

Sawai Gandharva (1886–1952)was a disciple of Ustad Abdul Karim Khan of the Kirana gharana. His famous disciples are Gangubai Hangal, Bhimsen Joshi and Firoze Dastur.

sawal jawab means question and answer. It is the term used for a technique where two instruments play together and seem to converse with each other. It also means the kind of figures that have at least a minimum of three notes being played one after another in two parts of the scale.

saz is an Urdu word which denotes instruments of accompaniment. The combination of harmonium or sarangi with the tanpura and the tabla form the saz of a performance in which the singer is the solo.

Senia gharana is the name of the line of musicians who have come through the tradition of

Mian Tansen. The word Sen was added to the names of those who came through this line.

shadava is a raga of six notes.

shadja is the very first note of the Indian scale. This note therefore becomes the tonic note and is an ACHALA SWARA. Its nature includes all the various techniques of voice production using head and chest and dental, humming and sinus notes. It is called shadja as it has all the succeeding six notes of the scale incipient within it and one of the techniques of swarasadhana is intended to make it possible for the practitioner to produce six distinct positions within that single note.

Sham Chaurasi is the name of a gharana of musicians from the little town of Sham Chaurasi near Hoshiarpur in the Punjab. Ustad Salamat Ali Khan who lived in Pakistan is its only musician still living.

shankh is the conch shell used in worship. When blown through its narrow end it produces an eerie blowing sound that in ancient times was used in war. It is among the many symbols that denote Lord Vishnu.

shehnai is a clarinet kind of wind instrument somewhat like the nagaswaram of the Carnatic system and is played in a celebratory vein. Its sound is deemed to be auspicious. The father of the shehnai in recent times is Ustad Bismilla Khan.

shishya means a disciple. 'Shish' means to punish indicating the punishingly difficult period of the student's life. It also means to remind the student of the knowledge revived and preserved as part of the guru's inheritance.

shlok is a Sanskrit term meaning poetry, usually of

four lines.

shringara is one of the nava rasas and indicates love.

shruti constitutes the microtonal intervals between notes. The word shruti is made up of two parts: 'shru' meaning to hear and 'tina' which is to involve or use. A sound that is audible is a shruti and the Indian musical scale has twenty-two shrutis. The seven notes have innumerable shrutis, several of which are difficult to identify except in an emotional or in a psychological sense. While mathematical positioning of these notes can be done, the linguistic basis of Indian music makes these microtonal intervals a part of the language and its utterance in speech. The twenty-two shrutis have the following names: Siddha, Prabhavati, Kantha, Suprabha, Shikha, Diptimati, Ugra, Hladi, Nirviri, Dira, Sarphara,

Kshanti, Hridayonmulini, Visarini, Prasuna, Vibhuti, Malini, Chapala, Vala, Sarvaratna, Sitantaj, Vikalini.

shruti veena was a medieval instrument with twenty-two strings, each tuned to the shrutis of the scale. It was Sarangadeva who gave this instrument its name.

Siddheswari Devi (1903–1977) was a well known and magically gifted thumri singer of the Benares gharana. She was a disciple of Bade Ramdas and her name was a symbol of style and quality in the thumri genre. Among her many distinguished disciples are her daughter Savita Devi, Rita Ganguly, B. Sushila and many others.

sitar is one of the most popular of Indian musical instruments. Its name has Persian roots in which 'seh' meant three and 'taar' meant strings. The old 'sehtar' had three strings. (See also MASIT KHAN.)

solkattu is the term denoting the mnemonics of dance.

Sriranjani is a Carnatic raga of the twenty-second mela, Karaharapriya (Kafi thaat). It is a shadava-shadava raga.

srot means a current or a continuously flowing body of water or a fountain. It describes the continually flowing quality of music. Its largely spiritual connotation lies in this word.

sthayi is the opening movement of a bandish.

stotra is a Sanskrit couplet describing the deity of worship. The root of the word is 'stu' which means the very essence of a deity. A stuti on the other hand, is a poem of praise of the deity but not a description.

Subhapantuvarali is a Carnatic raga of the forty-fifth melakarta. It belongs to the Todi thaat.

suddha means pure or untainted. The standard scale with its flat notes are called suddha swaras.

Sultan Husein Sirki (1458–1499) lived in Jaunpur and was among the foremost singers of his time and discovered ragas like Jaunpuri, Sindhura and Shyam.

surbahar is a large sitar whose strings are thick and whose frets are heavy. Its tone is deep and its technique is identical to that used for the sitar. For alap, jor and jhala, this instrument has a special dignity of tone and texture that is curiously attractive.

Surdas (1535–1640) was among the greatest poets of the Hindi language. He was a devotee of Lord Krishna. The raga Surdasi Malhar is believed to have been discovered by him. Legend has it that he blinded himself so that his eyes may not fall upon any material object, and he could meditate on Krishna. Surdas was born with the name of Bilwa Mangal and made a vow that he would compose a hundred and fifty thousand songs in praise of Lord Krishna. He died before reaching his goal and his disciples completed his vow writing under the name of Surshyam.

Suresh Babu Mane (1902–1953), popularly referred to as just Suresh Babu, was a disciple of Ustad Abdul Karim Khan and also of Ustad Abdul Wahid Khan. He was Hirabai Barodekar's brother. His voice was a soft and appealing one and bore a close resemblance to that of his guru Abdul Karim Khan. Prabha Atre, the well-known contemporary singer, is a disciple of Suresh Babu.

Swami Haridas is said to have been born in 1512. Nobody knows where he was actually born. He was a saintly man and lived a great part of his life in the environs of Vrindavan near the river Yamuna. He was a strict explorer of the world of nada yoga and possessed the most magical voice. He was a dhrupad singer and among his shishyas the names of Baiju Bawra, Gopal Lal, Ramdas and Ram Tanu are the most well known. Ram Tanu became famous as Tansen in the court of Akbar. Right up to our times the memory of Swami Haridas is venerated in Mathura and music conferences are held in his memory.

swara is described as a note. In actual fact the swara is not a note. The note is an instrumental or mechanical sound. The swara, on the other hand, is always a human utterance. Instruments, when playing swaras, have to be specially trained to produce the imitation of a vocal sound. The word has its roots in Sanskrit in which 'swa' stands for self and 'ra' stands for shining forth. Thus it is a sound in which the self must shine forth. Ragas are not made from notes but from swaras.

swara bheda is a technique of modal shift of the tonic note.

swara lipi is the notation or the score of a musical composition. Lipi is writing and therefore the writing of the swara is the term's literal translation.

Swaramela Kalanidhi is a grantha on Carnatic music composed by Ramamathya Pandit in 1550. It contains an elaborate analysis of the melas of Carnatic ragas.

swara murchchana is the term describing the scales derived from the Sa grama, the Ga grama and the Ma grama, with each scale emerging from the Sa, Ga and Ma as tonic notes. It is the modal to all these three notes.

swara panchama is the fifth note of the scale. It has no flat or sharp variants and is hence an ACHALA swara.

swara prasthara is an exercise of arpeggios or phrases of notes in various rhythms and layas of the solfege or sargams of the raga. The technique is a play on scales and creates a lot of excitement in the audience. It is very popular in Carnatic music.

swayambhu gandhara is heard as a resonance in the lowest tonic note or shadja in a tanpura or even in voices that have been trained in the traditional manner.

Syama Shastri (1762–1827) is regarded as one of Carnatic music's trinity. His name was Venkata Subramanya, but he was nicknamed Shyama. He was born in Tiruvarur in Tanjore district. The distinct technical characteristic of his compositions, their feeling and profundity and the sense of spiritual aura made his contribution to Carnatic music exceptional and immortal.

T

taan is the word that describes certain musical figures in which the notes have designs and patterns that grow at various speeds. An arpeggio of Western music would be a taan in Indian classical music. There are two major classifications of taans: shuddha taan and koot taan. There are 49 shuddha taans and 5048 koot taans possible. The names of the various taan types are shuddh or sapat, mishra taan, phirat ki taan, chhoot taan, jabre ki taan and halak ki taan.

taar means the strings of a musical instrument.

taar shehnai is an esraj filled with a small device which produces the sound effect of a shehnai.

tabla is the most popular percussion instrument of Hindustani music. It consists of a pair of drums, of which one is the treble (dayan) and the other the bass (bayan). Together they produce a fine texture of sound. The dhrupad and the dhammar alone use the pakhawaj. All other forms of Hindustani classical music use the tabla. The basic tonic note is tuned on the right drum and the left is tuned to an octave below. This kind of double drum combination is believed to have been devised by Hazrat Amir Khusro.

tabla taranga is a collection of about fifteen tablas tuned to the treble of the notes of the scale. It is played by striking its surface with both hands.

tala is often described as rhythm in English. Tala is not rhythm; it is part of language and the spoken cadences of poetry. It is defined in terms of matras in repeating cycles of beats that expand to a stressed point called the sam down to a release point called khali.

Some well-known and commonly used talas are as follows:

(i) **Adi tala** is a cycle of eight matras in the Carnatic system of music. Its beats fall on the first, the fifth and the seventh matras.

(ii) **Chautal** has twelve matras and is played on the pakhawaj. Its beats are on the fifth, ninth, and the eleventh matras. It has two khali matras—the third and the seventh.

(iii) **Dadra** is a cycle of six matras largely used in light music such as thumris and bhajans. Its bol is *dha dhi na dhi ti na*.

(iv) **Deepchandi** has fourteen matras used in thumri and other light forms. It is also known as **Chachar**.

Its bol is *dha dhin dhin, dha dha tin tin, ta tin tin, dha dha dhin dhin*.

(v) **Dhammar** has fourteen matras and is played on the pakhawaj. This tala accompanies dhrupad singing. Its bol is *ke dhita dhita dha aa, ke tit tit ta aa*.

(vi) **Ektal** has twelve beats and is played on the tabla. Its bol is *dhin dhin dhage tirkit, tu na kat ta, dhage tirkit, dhi na na*. This tala is the tabla equivalent of the chautal played on the pakhawaj.

(vii) **Jhumra** is a tala of fourteen matras. Its divisions are 3-4, 3-4. Its beats are on the first, the fourth and the eleventh. The khali is on the eighth matra. Its bol is *dhin na, dha tirkit, dhin dhin, dha ge tirkit, tin na, ta tirkit dhin dhin, dha ge tirkit*.

(viii) **Jhaptal** has ten matras. Its bol is *dhi na dhi dhi na, ti na ti ti na*.

(ix) **Keherwa** is a tala of four matras. Its bol is *dha gi na tinaka dhi na*.

(x) **Rupak** is a tala of seven matras and its bol is *tin tin na dhi na dhi na*.

(xi) **Sulfakta** or **Sul tala** has seven matras. Its bol is *dha dha dhin ta, kit dha, kit taka gadi gana*. It is mostly played on the pakhawaj for dhrupad compositions.

(xii) **Sawari** has an odd number of matras. There are two kinds of sawari: a fifteen-matra sawari and a nineteen-matra sawari.

(xiii) **Tin Tala** is the most popular tala in Hindustani music and there are a large number of compositions in this tala. It has sixteen matras with beats on the first, fifth and thirteenth matras. Its khali is on the ninth matra.

tala vadya is an orchestrated performance of several percussion instruments. Tabla, pakhawaj, mridangam, ghatam, kanjira, moorsing are all included, played together, building up to a crescendo and then releasing the tension.

taleem is the process of learning or teaching in the guru-shishya tradition.

Talwandi is the name of a gharana. It is a small town in the neighbourhood of Hoshiarpur in the Punjab. This gharana is no longer extant. Its principal musicians were Maula Baksh and Meher Ali and a well-known clarinet player named Khaira.

tambura (tanpura) is a drone instrument usually with four strings. Its two middle strings are tuned to the singing pitch of the performer or player. The two other strings are tuned one to the fifth or the fourth below the pitch and the fourth string is tuned to the tonic of the octave below.

tandava is a word that is derived from the cosmic dance of the creator and destroyer of the universe, Lord Shiva. It relates both to creation and to destruction. It is the most well-known pose of the Lord Shiva and is the central posture of Shiva in the temples of India, particularly in the south. This pose is a very basic element in dance. There are several tandavas like the Gauri tandava, Tripura tandava, Kalika tandava, Ananda tandava—all various forms of the concept of tandava.

Tanna Mishra was the earlier name of Mian Tansen. The son of Makarand Misra of Benares, the young Tanna was gifted with an extraordinary vocal timbre. He was trained under Swami Haridas of Brindawan and soon rose to countrywide fame as Tansen in the court of Emperor Akbar where he adorned the court as one of his navaratnas. Among the most legendary of Hindustani classical musicians, Tansen is reported to have made several ragas which have the prefix of 'Mian ki' and several dhrupads. His voice is believed to have produced rain and thunder, lit fires and controlled wild animals.

tanpura is a drone instrument with four strings, three of steel and the fourth of brass. This is the basic and the most vital of Indian classical musical instruments. This instrument is tuned usually to the tonic and its fourth or fifth or even the seventh.

Tansen is the name of Tanna Mishra, the great singer in the court of Emperor Akbar.

tappa is one of the lighter classical styles from the Punjab, sung in its folk forms by cowherds and camel drivers. Its language is rural and the double note fast passages with which its text is filled makes it a difficult technique to master. Gulam Nabi Mian made this style popular. These songs have love and separation as their principal themes.

tarab are the sympathetic strings that are attached beneath and on the side of instruments like the sitar, the sarod, the sarangi and so on. These are each tuned to each of the frets and resonate when the note is struck or when the harmonics are played. This gives tonal richness to the notes of these instruments.

tarana is a composition in which mnemonics are used, which are meaningless syllables that extrapolate the raga and produce rhythmic delight. Since the letters used in them have no meaning, the technique serves only a rhythmic purpose. Syllables *tana*, *dir*, *dani*, *tadani* and Persian syllables *alayi illa*, and several others like *nom tom* and so on are used. Hazrat Amir Khusro is believed to have originated this kind of composition.

tara saptak is the octave immediately above that of the basic melody.

taseer means impact on the mind and the emotions.

tasha is a tiny earthenware drum tied to the chest and played with sticks. This is played during the Muslim observance of Muharram.

tatkar involves the use of feet in training for dance in the same way as the voice is exercised through the swara in song and the fingers are trained to play instruments. These exercises, which are part of the basic alphabets of dance, are called tatkar.

teevra is the first in the twenty-two shruti classification. It can also be classified as the sharp tone following a flat tone.

thaat is the name given to the ragas which Pandit Vishnu Narayan Bhatkhande selected out of the seventy melakartas of the Carnatic system to constitute the main ragas from which all others are derived. There are ten thaats based on the Venkatmukhi approach and is now universally accepted in Hindustani classical music. These thaats have the names of ragas and these ten are Bilawal, Khamaj, Poorvi, Kafi, Bhairavi, Kalyan, Bhairav, Marwa, Asavari, and Todi.

theka is the structure associated with the simple statement of a single cycle or avarta of a tala. This word is associated with the mridang, pakhawaj and the tabla and the other tala percussion instruments. The mnemonics associated with the theka constitute the simplest description of the tala in its ordinary expression. The theka covers the cycle and can be counted to contain the basic number of matras of the tala of which it is the theka.

thumri has a preeminent place among light classical musical varieties. Composed in the Khari bolis like Bhojpuri and Brij, the thumri is a highly popular form. Among the styles of thumri singing, the Punjabi and the Lucknavi are the most predominant. The thumri is often in the Punjabi tala, a kind of teen tala. There are several ragas in which thumris are sung and its delicacy and appeal are obtained by a judicious mix of ragas.

Thyagaraja (1767–1847) is the most effulgent of the Carnatic musical trinity. Born in Tiruvarur in Tanjore district, he was the son of a Brahmin scholar in Sanskrit and Telugu, well-versed in the Vedas, astrology and mantra shastra. His immense poetics and profound understanding of the essence of bhakti made his music a powerful force in Carnatic music.

tigun is thrice the standard madhya laya tempi, that is for each matra it has three aksharas.

tihayi is the technique that repeats a phrase three times to the accented beat of a tala cycle. The division of any tala into three equal parts to conclude a variation is called tihayi. (See also MOHARA.)

tillana is a Carnatic tarana. These tillanas are brilliant tala configurations that use mnemonic syllables like the tarana such as *Na, Dir, Tar, Tilla, Na* and so on.

tilwada is a tala of sixteen matras divided into four equal sections. The first beat is the sam. The second beat is on the fifth matra, the ninth is the empty beat or the khali and the final beat is on the thirteenth matra.

tirvat is a composition that has mnemonics like the tarana. Swarashabda and the bols of the pakhawaj are incorporated in its structure. This kind of composition has rarely been sung in recent decades.

trital is a sixteen matra tala which is among the most popular rhythm measures. Its popularity lies in the fact that its gait is divided into four equal measures of four matras each, so that the first, the fifth and the thirteenth have beats and the ninth is the unaccented open beat or khali.

Tukaram was a saint of Maharashtra whose bhajans and poetry are widely sung to this day.

tukda literally means a

piece. These are swara or tala sections that are often played at twice or four and eight times the basic beat. They are added to the main tala cycles to explore the varieties of mathematical variations of the basic interval of time in which the main composition is played.

Tulsidas was a saint whose adoration of Rama was of the same intensity as that of his Carnatic counterpart Thyagaraja. His *Ramcharitmanas* has moulded the spiritual and psychological world of the Hindi heartland of India as no other single work could be said to have done. Recited by every wandering sanyasi and mendicant, read by every literate Hindi-speaking Indian and sung in congregations as bhajans, Tulsidas is a household name all over India. Among the finest singers of the Tulsidas bhajans, Kumar Gandharva is considered the most evocative and his Long Playing Record entitled 'Tulsi-Ek Darshan' has brought the bhajans of Tulsidas into a novel focus.

U

uccharan would mean in musical terms the enunciation of a note, not merely its pronunciation.

udatta is the highest note in the three-note chant of the Vedas. The lowest is called anudatta and the remaining note is the swarita.

upaj is the trained creative impulse which uses the rules of the art to create new and fresh nuances each time music is sung or played, and has added to it a continuity of uninterrupted inspiration.

ustad really means a maestro. The conventional practice is to use the title for Muslim musicians and the word 'pandit' for Hindu musicians.

uttar mandra is the first murcchana of the shadja grama. Its sequence is as follows: *Sa, Re, Ga, Ma, Pa, Dha, Ni, Sa, Ni, Dha, Pa, Ma, Ga, Re, Sa.*

uttarang is the upper tetrachord of the scale, the portion beyond the madhyam.

V

vadi is a word that has its root in vad' which means to speak. It is a note in the scale of a raga that is evocative and produces the feeling of the raga. It is usually positioned in the lower tetrachord and has its consonant note in the upper tetrachord called the samavadi. Both together constitute points of tension and intensity on the raga scale and play a pivotal role in making a raga come alive.

vadya is any musical instrument. Since raga music is voice-based, vadya constitutes a method of conversation between singer and his accompanist and hence the root 'vad' which is an exchange of words.

vaggeyakar is a composer and a creator of music 'Vagge' is drawn from the root 'vaak' meaning to speak, 'geya' is to sing and 'kaar' is the craftsman. The word would therefore coaelsce to mean one who composes a song and sings it.

vairagya is the psychological state of detachment from worldly concerns. It is the state of mind of one who has developed a certain distance from the ordinary attachments that bedevil existence. In music it is a kind of performance in which the singer himself does not participate in the evocative content of his music but is able to produce startling responses in his listeners.

vakra really means twisted or non regular. It indicates a break of continuity or regularity in the accepted order of notes in the aroha-avarohana of ragas.

vakra aroha is an ascending series of notes that do not move in a regular and predictable fashion.

vakra avarohana is the absence of a predetermined order in a series of descending notes.

Vakulabharanam belongs in the fourteenth melakarta, Dhati Vasantha Bhairavi. There is no raga of this name in Hindustani music. It can be produced by combining Bhairav and Bhairavi in poorvanga and uttaranga respectively.

vani means the sayings of saints. For example, the Gurubani consists of the words of saints and gurus. Vani in the Carnatic tradition refers to a musical style such as the vani of Tiger Varadachari or Chembai. The word does not mean a gharana in the Hindustani music sense but has a similar connotation.

varna literally means colour. It could also mean a category. In music the word would mean a quality of perception in a swara or a phrase which is psychologically rather than physically audible.

veena is any stringed instrument, in the sense that it produces musically meaningful sound. The number of veenas in music are many—dattatraya veena, saraswati veena, vichitra veena, rudra veena and so on. Even the human body is likened to a musical instrument when fully trained and is often referred to as gatra veena.

vidwan is the generic term used for a scholar. In the Carnatic tradition it refers to a musician who not merely sings but is also a master of his art.

vidyut taan is an arpeggio or a series of swaras in motion that is likened to lightning or is as fast as electricity.

vikrut swara is the name given to all those notes of a scale that have a flat or a sharp. In the Indian scale, except for the fifth and the tonic notes that have no sharp or flat, all positions of a note that deviate from the standard flat form are called vikrut. These notes are the rishabh, the gandhara, the madhyam, the dhaivat and the nishad.

vikrut taan is used in the stylistic sense of being complicated in its design and configuration, its speed and laya quality, its tension and tightness of traverse, its trajectory and so on.

Vilabal is the Hindustani equivalent of the Carnatic Dheera Shankarabharanam and is the diatonic scale. It has all the seven notes and all of these are suddha swaras. In the Carnatic scale this is a melakarta and in the Hindustani scale this is a thaat.

vilambit refers to the slow tempi composition that is also called bada khayal. 'Vilamb' means long in the sense of time. (See also LAYA.)

Vilayat Husein Khan (1862–1962) was from the Agra gharana. He was a musician and composer of note and a scholar. He has several khayal compositions to his credit in which he uses the signature, Prana Piya. He also wrote a treatise named *Sangeetagyan Samskaran* in which he discusses the musicians of his time.

Vishnu Digambar Palusker (1872–1931) was among the greatest savants of the Gwalior gharana. He was the disciple of Balakrishna Buwa Inchalkaranjiker. Palusker made every effort to popularise classical music. He sent out musical evangelists to teach in schools. Among his chief flag bearers were Pandit V.A. Kashalker, Pandit Onkarnath Thakur, V.N. Patwardhan, Narayan Rao Vyas and B.R.Deodhar. His son was Dattatraya Palusker, who was among the youngest and the most popular musicians of his time. He, unfortunately, died young.

Vishrambari is the seventeenth melakarta of Carnatic music.

Vishwambari is the fifty-fourth melakarta of Carnatic music whose old name was Vamshawali. This raga bears a resemblance to Pooriya Dhanasri.

vistar is to elaborate, expand, and explore the true spirit of a raga.

vivadi swara is a swara in a scale that is prohibited in a raga and is therefore to be omitted.

vrinda gana is choral singing.

W

Wajid Ali Shah (1823–1887) was the last nawab of Oudh. He was a great lover of music and a special devotee of the thumri form. It was under the signature of Akhtar Piya that he composed many thumris. A devotee of the Lord Krishna, he supported many singers of his time who became masters of the thumri, among whom Kalka Bindadin was the foremost.

Y

Yadukula Kambhoji comes from the twenty-eighth melakarta Harikambhoji which is the Khamaj thaat of Hindustani music. There is no raga in Hindustani music with this name.

yakshagana is a folk dance-drama of South and North Kanara districts of Karnataka. It has a combination of dance and music and its stories are taken from the Puranas and deal with the ten incarnations of Vishnu. Its origin is somewhat uncertain. Perhaps it goes as far as back as the Kannada poet Ratnakara Varni of 1557 AD although other writers like Shivarama Karanth say that it has at least a 1000 years of history.

Yeman is also called Kalyan or Kalyani. It belongs to the Kalyan thaat or Mechha Kalyani in Carnatic music which is the sixty-fifth melakarta. It is an evening raga in Hindustani music.

Yeman Kalyan is also called Jaimini Kalyan. It is slightly different from raga Yeman. It belongs to the Kalyan thaat or the Mechhakalyani in Caranatic music. The shuddha madhyam is used in the raga of Yeman to make it Yeman Kalyan. Its use needs the highest musical subtlety to produce the effect of the raga on the mind.

Z

zamin is the ground or the basic structure and paradigm of the raga under elaboration.

zamzama is the musical technique of shaking a note back and forth It is a grace.

zigar is musical temperament in the sense of emotional content.